THE RISE OF GLADSTONE TO THE
LEADERSHIP OF THE
LIBERAL PARTY
1859 to 1868

THE RISE OF GLADSTONE
TO THE
LEADERSHIP OF THE
LIBERAL PARTY
1859 to 1868

BY

W. E. WILLIAMS, M.A.
Late Scholar of Peterhouse

"The past is well nigh really past, and a
new policy and a wiser and a higher
morality are sighed for by the best of our
people, and there is a prevalent feeling
that *you* are destined to guide that wiser
policy and to teach that higher morality."
BRIGHT to GLADSTONE. 1 Jan. 1861.

CAMBRIDGE
AT THE UNIVERSITY PRESS
1934

CAMBRIDGE
UNIVERSITY PRESS

University Printing House, Cambridge CB2 8BS, United Kingdom

Cambridge University Press is part of the University of Cambridge.

It furthers the University's mission by disseminating knowledge in the pursuit of education, learning and research at the highest international levels of excellence.

www.cambridge.org
Information on this title: www.cambridge.org/9781107456266

First published 1934
First paperback edition 2014

A catalogue record for this publication is available from the British Library

ISBN 978-1-107-45626-6 Paperback

CONTENTS

CONTENTS

PREFACE

THIS essay, which was awarded the Prince Consort Prize in 1932, is based on a study of the Gladstone Papers between 1859 and 1869. In setting out to do some research on the career of Gladstone, I was guided by Professor G. M. Trevelyan, who suggested that it might be possible to do some profitable work on the last years of Lord Palmerston and the Second Reform Bill, in order to follow Gladstone's development in this critical middle period of his career. Accordingly I sought permission to consult the Gladstone Papers, and this great privilege was granted me by Mr H. N. Gladstone (now Lord Gladstone of Hawarden). Having gained access to the documents, however, one's feet were not yet on the high road, for the bulk of the material was enormous. Signal help of two kinds made it possible to proceed.

The first was Lord Morley's *Life of Gladstone*. When he began the task of examining the Hawarden Papers, Morley said that he had only encountered so vast a store in one other place and that was at Dublin Castle. There was scarcely any name bearing any kind of reputation, English or foreign, which did not figure in the list of Mr Gladstone's correspondents. Through this wilderness of documents, Morley drove a highway and produced one of the great permanent English biographies. Upon this book, almost all subsequent work on Gladstone depends. However deep the sense of debt to Morley while reading his printed word, it was eclipsed by the realisation of the genius of his pioneer work. There is hardly a paper of any importance (in the period under consideration) which does not bear Morley's pencil mark. His survey, his course and his selection are always unerring.

Apart from the general obligation to Lord Morley's *Life*, I was helped in the second place, as all Gladstone students must be, by the work of Mr A. Tilney-Bassett, who arranged this vast collection of private papers in boxes labelled with the correspondents' names, with every letter in its correct chronological place, supplying, in addition, an elaborate series of references to the whole correspondence. The rough rule of thumb, then, in beginning the research, was to read through the boxes of letters from Cobden, Bright, Russell, Clarendon, Forster and so on. Since I began this work the Gladstone Papers have been transferred from Hawarden to the British Museum, but they have not yet (1933) been officially numbered. I have therefore placed a marginal number at the beginning of every letter quoted, and also made a list of these letters in the Appendix. Short quotations are marked with an asterisk. In making a selection from the Gladstone Papers I have sought to use letters which show the kind of influence or pressure which was brought to bear upon Gladstone between 1859 and 1868.

I wish to thank Lord Gladstone of Hawarden for giving me permission to consult the Papers and for his interest in the progress of this study. To Mr A. Tilney-Bassett I owe a great debt for his assistance at every stage and with every problem connected with the correspondence.

PREFACE

From the beginning I have been guided and helped by the criticisms and suggestions of Professor G. M. Trevelyan of Trinity College and Professor H. W. V. Temperley of Peterhouse, and I am very grateful to them both. My thanks are also due to Mr G. A. Jones of Birkenhead for help in making transcripts and to the staff of the Liverpool Picton Library.

A research student could not undertake this type of work without generous assistance from various bodies. In this connection I beg to acknowledge my deep obligation to the Master and Fellows of Peterhouse, the Goldsmiths' Company of London and the Education Authority of the City of Stoke-on-Trent.

W. E. W.

Birkenhead
January 1934

CHAPTER I

INTRODUCTION. THE PROBLEM. AUTHORITIES

"Anyone who wishes to make out a case against Gladstone should fix on 1865 rather than on 1885 for his study."

Francis Birrell, *Gladstone*, p. 71.

ONE of the most remarkable things about the supply of information we possess on the career of Gladstone is the fact that it is very unevenly distributed along the length of his career. If we adopt Maitland's method with our Morley and work towards the source, we find ourselves exploring a kind of literary St Lawrence. The long and broad estuary of Home Rule is connected with those great lakes of information on Canning and Peel, where the stream is born, by what is, in comparison, a very narrow channel. The phenomenon is readily explained, partly by the life of Gladstone, partly by the life of the biographer himself. What is not so easily explained is this: that since the publication of Morley's *Life of Gladstone*, the structure of his narrative has been elaborated, but its design remains unchanged. The middle portion, Book v of the work, between 1859 and 1868, is still slender; indeed it seems to have shrunk compared with the monstrous proportions of the ends. Closer examination shows that the problem is not peculiar to the *Life of Gladstone*; indeed, it opens a more profound question. Is it not the tendency, in English historical writing on the nineteenth century, to neglect investigation of the 'sixties? Some vague hints have been thrown out that it was an age of slow motion; in fact, many of the standard histories tell us frankly that the nation was not only at the halt, but that it was standing at ease. In politics after 1860 and before 1866, Palmerston is spoken of alternately as a barrier and a dam. But the mere theory of stagnation, and it is a mistaken one, is not sufficient to explain why so little has been written on this middle period. A truer explanation is, that it is the meeting place of two political generations. No recorder would spend much time in describing the instant in a relay race when the flag was being handed over. The historians have concentrated on the times, before and after, when the race was in full progress. A great generation was passing away; and many of its great successors were still unknown men. Between 1860 and 1865 England lost Palmerston, Herbert, Cobden and Lewis; it was common knowledge that Russell's political life was near its close. The parliamentary mettle of the new men, Northcote, Granville, Harcourt and Goschen, had scarcely been tested. Historical writers, and they are now chiefly biographers to the detriment of the subject, realised that the period would offer them little of the spectacular. The reapers warned the gleaners; we have been cheated of the historical study and of the memoir and the reminiscence.[1]

The tendency grows to overwork the 'thirties and 'forties and the 'eighties and the 'nineties, and to leave the middle period to take care of itself. We know of no

---

[1] E.g. M. Halévy followed up his work on the Chartist Period with a volume on the Trade Unions of the 'nineties.

other century in English history where this charge could be preferred; the noblest example of even distribution is the seventeenth. In the nineteenth century the account of some decades has become dropsical. Defence, on the grounds that the 'sixties lacked the incident, the colour and the intensity of other years, is untenable. In the world of science alone, the middle years rank with the age of Faraday and of Huxley; they include, in foreign politics, consummations of the greatest importance, and at home, at least one state paper of the first rank which has never earned its due publicity, and the birth of one of the most powerful political parties England has ever seen. The cry, then, that the old politicians, novelists, journalists and raconteurs were dead or dying; that their successors were still apprentices, rings falsely. The historian must appear, if the general design of English historical writing is not to be impaired; if the history of a century can still be written by one man, who will treat the information amassed at the beginning and at the end as piers, on which to rest the long bridge of his narrative. Grant, but for a moment, that there was an interregnum. Then the three men who became political regents must stand out in bold relief. No one can complain that the biographies of Disraeli and Bright, at this juncture, lack the adequate fullness. It is when we come to accounts of Gladstone that we find the hiatus.

The explanation lies, first, in the life of Gladstone. His early years are, in a very real sense, the key to the whole; his later years are "magnificent and stormy". He began political life when the rotten boroughs were still offering to young men of birth or ability the opportunity of entering Parliament. They were placed under a political tutor to read. The statesmen who began their careers before the Great Reform Bill was passed frequently spoke of themselves as the pupils of the ministers they found in office or as "being bred under the shadow of a great name". Gladstone began work at this period. The influence of Canning and of Peel, no less than the influence of Oxford, must be examined thoroughly, and they explain why the source is bountiful. The ample conclusion is no less a matter of politics. We would have expected any biographer to dwell at length on the fourth and fifth acts of the long drama. After the close of the first Liberal ministry, Gladstone had almost achieved that unparalleled position in English life which he occupied for twenty years. His character and his acts, viewed from whatever angle, make him the peer of the greatest English statesmen. No sixteenth-century reformer wielded more power over his adherents or roused more savage hatred in the haunts of privilege than did the leader of the Liberal party. His followers in Manchester, or in Bradford or in Wrexham, became zealots with all the paraphernalia of a religion. They had their priest, and if the oracle was sometimes perplexing, it only served to intensify the blind adherence. And if there never were such a priest, there never were such disciples. The working-man Liberal, particularly if he was a nonconformist, gave to the party a strength and a devotion which has never been surpassed. The fire was fanned by a type of newspaper which it is difficult now to believe ever existed in England. The editor wrote for men who were genuinely interested in politics. No one can open the files of any English provincial newspaper between 1860 and 1890 without being struck by the character of the news. Foreign policy was discussed with a detail which a university class would now find overpowering; the clauses of treaties and bills were printed. This is true of provincial newspapers published in industrial towns, where the circulation could not depend on a leisured or a cultured class. In this atmosphere Gladstone fought some tremendous and spectacular issues; his Irish policy alone warrants the length at which his biographer has treated his career after 1870. Leader, followers and affairs were at full tide then.

And secondly, the biographer could scarcely help himself. In writing on the Home Rule period, his authority was unquestioned. He had borne the burden and the heat of the day and he had read the documents afterwards—a rare experience for the historian. The world expected Morley to say much about Ireland in his book, and the world was not disappointed. We know now that he was bound to be equally diffident when speaking of the 'sixties.[1] Between 1860 and 1870, his contempt of the politics of the hour knew no bounds. Finding a ready listener in Frederic Harrison, he poured out his complaints about "the political stagnation". No statesman satisfied his radicalism. When he wrote in the *Fortnightly Review* (September, 1868) under the title "Old Parties and New Policy"—"Take Mr Mill and Mr Bright out of the lower house, and there is probably

[1] It has been suggested that Lord Morley was not particularly interested in this period.

about as much political genius and administrative power in the foremost men of one chamber as there is in the foremost men of the other "—he was still unregenerate. He had not recognised his master in Gladstone. When he came to write on this period, the experience was embarrassing, and he faltered.

Such we believe to be the reasons why the classic *Life of Gladstone* becomes inadequate at the period of the struggle over the Second Reform Bill. In an unaccountable manner, amounting almost to conspiracy, other books have ignored and perpetuated the defect. The diaries of John Bright and Stafford Northcote take us to the fringe of the Second Reform Bill—one of the cardinal points in Gladstone's career—and then stop short, resuming after the struggle is over. The dearth of accounts by eye-witnesses, such as Macaulay in one age and Lucy in another, leaves us equally windbound.[1] The sources of secondary value after 1870 are bewildering in their extent; and there is hardly a man or woman who could handle a pen who has not left us some portrait of the veteran Gladstone.

The most detailed accounts of the 'sixties can be found in the valuable *History of Twenty-Five Years* by Spencer Walpole and the five volumes of Mr Herbert Paul. In addition we have the standard biographies, Morley's *Lives* of Gladstone and Cobden, Dasent's *Life of Delane*, Hobson's *Cobden, the International Man*, and the official lives of Disraeli, Granville and Bright. There are two or three old books on the Second Reform Bill which have

---

[1] There is valuable contemporary evidence, however, in the Diary of Mr Speaker Denison.

not been superseded, notably those by Heaton (*The Three Reforms of Parliament*) and Cox (*The Second Reform Bill*). One of the finest studies on the period is F. E. Gillespie's *Labour and Politics in England*, 1850 *to* 1867, which goes at length into the question of the artisan and parliamentary reform with elaborate documentation. The supply of printed letters and papers increases from year to year. For the problems of the period, *The Later Correspondence of Lord John Russell* by Dr Gooch, and *Palmerston and Gladstone* (The Palmerston Papers) by Mr Guedalla, are invaluable.

Yet there are many problems in the career of Gladstone between 1860 and 1868, which need fuller discussion. For example, Gladstone's declaration on Baines's Bill in 1864 never seems to have been analysed completely. Morley is very restrained at this point. The real question is, how did Gladstone arrive at this position, and how far did he mean what he said? What was Gladstone's temper in the first six months of 1866, and what men were bringing influence to bear upon him? It is certain that he made great strides towards the modern Liberal position between 1863 and 1868. We have to discover and estimate the forces, particularly that of the working class. The episodes of the transition can be summed up under the following heads: the relations between Gladstone and Cobden, notably over the Commercial Treaty; what was said and thought of Gladstone's future by contemporaries; his relations with great boroughs after 1863; what the real effect was of the death of Lord Palmerston. Is it true that "1865 was the only time when Gladstone embarked on a change of policy which redounded to his immediate advantage "?[1] And in conclusion what effects had the Irish Church Resolutions and the General Election of 1868 on the future of Liberalism? In elucidating the development of Gladstone's opinions during these years and the forces which were working upon him, we shall have the surest key to interpret the Reform Struggle of 1866 and 1867. Who or what slipped the muzzle, and why did the interest in reform suddenly blaze up after the Liberal resignation in 1866? These questions have been before the mind during the search through the Gladstone Papers, and the letters, at least, provide the background to the whole period, and will, I believe, help to explain why "the Gladstone of 1865, felt quite a different person from the Gladstone of 1859".[2] The gradualness of the change was characteristic. In the Resolutions on the Irish Church, he said of those who thought an establishment hallowed, "There may be those who think that to lay hands upon the constitution is a profane and unhallowed act. I respect that feeling. I sympathise with it, while I think it my duty to overcome and repress it". He might have said the same thing in 1866 in addressing the opponents of parliamentary reform.

[1] Francis Birrell, *Gladstone*, p. 71.
[2] *Ibid*. p. 72.

CHAPTER II

ESTIMATES OF GLADSTONE, 1860–1868

"His first principles are rarely ours; we may often think them obscure—sometimes incomplete—occasionally quite false; but we cannot deny that they are the result of distinct thought with disciplined faculties upon adequate data, of a careful and dispassionate consideration of all the objections which occurred, whether easy or insuperable, trifling or severe."

W. Bagehot on Gladstone: Essay on "Oxford", 1852.

MORLEY arrested his narrative at a point in the middle of the 'sixties to describe the opinion of mankind on Gladstone. His future was one of the most perplexing problems of the age. It was admitted on all hands that he was a genius, but the very type of the admission was in itself a stumbling-block. Reputations cannot thrive on bouquets alone. Gladstone's post-bag from time to time grew heavy with letters of congratulation for some brilliant speech or for some outstanding example of mastery in debate. Here is a typical specimen from Clarendon, April 19th, 1853: "I will not take up your time by adding to the number 1 of congratulations you must already have received, for I could not in a few words, if at all, express my admiration of the most perfect financial statement ever heard within the walls of Parliament, for such it is allowed by friend and foe*". Tributes of this kind abounded, and they tended, to use a phrase of Dr Arnold's, to make Gladstone "dark from excess of brilliance". Could so rare a man

9

endure the drill and discipline of party? The newspapers and the great magazines thought not. They searched in vain for a label. Natural science always gives a place of honour to the specimen which cannot be classified, which breaks all the rules and which belongs to no family. It is not so in the science called politics. The man who is not easily ascribed to a particular species commits a misdemeanour; what is not readily understood can be as readily rejected. To politicians, journalists and club-men, Gladstone presented the incalculable. They could no more define his intellectual features than the carica-turists could draw Rosebery's face a generation later. Gladstone was not a "mystery man" in the sense in which Bright spoke of Disraeli's character, where springing surprises had become almost a matter of routine, and where men enjoyed the surprises for their own sake. This policy, frequently one of profound wisdom, though naturally dangerous in an assembly like the House of Commons and requiring personal gifts of the highest kind, never made any appeal to Gladstone. He baffled men by his explanations; he suffered from no more serious impediment than this. He had not learned the maxim "Never explain". Men looked for reasons from him because they had always been provided with them. But at the same time they received them without enthusiasm.

Three strains run through the criticism of his con-temporaries: they could not understand him; they never knew what he would do next; they had misgivings whether he would ever make a leader. Compared to his fellow-statesmen, his plight was grave; for they included two or three of the clearest cut personalities ever seen in English politics. Palmerston was transparent; Bright was hated because his aims were so unmistakable—to mention "the member for Birmingham" was to conjure up a real and lively vision. And even if Bagehot said that there had never been any one like Mr Cobden before, no one misunderstood his policy. These men stood out in bold relief; Gladstone remained immense and impenetrable.

Men could not understand him. The ablest critic of them all had some profound things to say on the mystery. Bagehot's opinion in 1860 expressed the general feeling of mankind: he sums up everything said or printed elsewhere in his quiet and authoritative manner. "It is necessary that England should comprehend Mr Gladstone. If the country have not a true conception of a great statesman, his popularity will be capricious, his power irregular and his usefulness insecure." There seems to have been a fair degree of unanimity over the elements of the mystery. Morley quotes some very wise words of Aberdeen: "when he has convinced himself, perhaps by abstract reasoning of some view, he thinks that every one else ought at once to see it as he does and can make no allowance for difference of opinion". Again, "He does not enough look out of the window".[1] Aberdeen's words were verified on many memorable occasions. The argument Gladstone produced in favour of taxation of charities was a monument of close reasoning; but it was the kind of argument, which, even in the House

---

[1] Morley, *Life of Gladstone*, vol. 1, p. 804. The references throughout are to the two-volume edition.

of Commons of that day, would tend to isolate its inventor. And in his noblest moment when defending Bradlaugh's cause, the voice was perhaps too Olympian. Gladstone's criticism of Robert Lowe is, however, a better description of himself in this direction, than any other. "Outstripping others in the race, you reach the goal before they do, and being there, assume that they are there also. This is unpopular."[1] In another valuable extract, Morley sets down the opinion of Mr Meredith Townsend in a number of the *Spectator* for 1864. This, one of the most remarkable and accurate political prophecies in our history, got at the root of the matter. "Mr Gladstone has done less to lay down any systematised course of action than almost any man of his political standing." Even with so difficult a subject, the critic foretold the direction of Gladstone's steps in foreign and domestic policy unerringly. Bagehot himself must take a second place here, though he did say, "Mr Gladstone is essentially a man who cannot impose his creed on his time, but must learn his creed of his time". The essayist knew that even this singular statesman must wait until the hour struck, and the journalist saw that he would be equal to the coming hour. We should give a false impression of the time if we listened to no other but these wise and restrained voices. The thinkers might warn, but the rank and file railed openly. Algernon West in his *Recollections*[2] gives us a picture of a man who was distrusted and disliked. "He was still, in 1868, looked upon by those who belonged to what were then called 'the

[1] Lord Oxford, *Fifty Years of Parliament*, vol. I, p. 17.
[2] Vol. II, p. 24.

governing families' of the country as an outsider. He was not bred in their kennel."

It was a fateful position for any man. "Quo vadis?" was on every tongue. There are two valuable letters from Dean Church (Morley made use of part of one) which, while moderate in tone, suggest the misgivings of the world.

"As you see, we have lost Palmerston. While he lived there was a tacit understanding that no internal battles of consequence were to be fought or great issues raised. The great interest is to see how Gladstone will comport himself. It is an awful time for him. The 'heart of all Israel is towards him'. He is very great and very noble. He has been the one man who has done any effective work in government lately. But he is hated as much as, or more than he is loved. He is fierce sometimes and wrathful and easily irritated. He wants knowledge of men and speaks rashly. And I look on with some trembling to see what will come of this his first attempt to lead the Commons and prove himself fit to lead England."[1]

Once more, writing in 1868, the Dean gives his testimony to support the feeling of many men on the uncertain position of the new leader. The Liberal party was notoriously wayward as Gladstone himself was forced to confess at the time.

"The change [i.e. the new Liberal ministry] has as yet made little difference to the world at large. But we have a ministry of newer blood and more detached from the old routine than any within living memory. The House of Commons on the other hand seems made up of much the same materials and Gladstone will have a tough job to keep it in order. There never was a man so genuinely admired for

[1] *Life and Letters of Dean Church*, p. 171, Nov. 1st, 1865.

the qualities which deserve admiration—his earnestness, his deep popular sympathies, his unflinching courage—and there never was a man more deeply hated, both for his good points and for undeniable defects and failings. But they love him much less in the House than they do out of doors." [This last judgment was very true; it is the supreme reason why Gladstone emerged so successfully from a decade of suspicion and mistrust.] "I will forward *The Times* on the chance when there is anything worth seeing. There is a curious and as far as I remember rather novel bit of popular enthusiasm in the hand-shaking at Windsor station of Gladstone and Bright—in a number which gives the account of the swearing in of the ministers." (Dean Church to Dr Gray, December 11th, 1868.)

Such was the view of a cleric. What did the statesmen think? Taking two examples, we must confess that the unhappy feeling of uncertainty was also shared by them. The one reference which Morley gives to Lowe[1] certainly demands some modification. "Lowe described [to Granville] as perfectly unjust and unfounded the criticism which had been made of your leadership." This was written on February 11th, 1867. And yet, only a year previously, in a letter to Henry Sherbrooke, Lowe had said, "Gladstone's failure as a leader becomes more manifest every day"[2] (February 20th, 1866). Lord Selborne's *Memorials*, though very different in temper from the turbulent story of Lowe's *Life*, echo the general opinion that Gladstone had failed to satisfy the examiners. "Gladstone would have been acknowledged by all to have done very well as a leader of the House of Commons,

[1] Vol. i, p. 806.
[2] Martin, *Life of Lord Sherbrooke*, vol. ii, p. 268.

14

if there had been no reform bill" [this was damning with faint praise; Roundell Palmer had missed the point so ably made by Mr Townsend—"all his speeches point to the inauguration of a new activity in all internal affairs"]. And he goes on to say, "But the responsibility for the management of this reform bill has lowered his prestige and upon the whole his success is dubious".[1]

It is interesting to compare this contemporary evidence with what has been written since. In this age of short biographies and so-called "studies" of the eminent, many attempts have been made to analyse Gladstone's mind and motives. Generally speaking, these attempts have failed because modern writers have been unable to bridge the gulf which separates us from the Victorian character, and have to content themselves with firing a few rockets across it. Epigrams entertain, but they leave the facts untouched. The attempt to reduce Gladstone to a set of formulae has most certainly failed. Be as clever as you may, the great facts of zealous churchmanship, of a sincere belief in Divine Providence, of a profound and intricate knowledge of affairs both political and economic (to name at random a few of Gladstone's qualities) still stand foursquare to all the winds that blow, as great as they ever were. Could any sentence reveal a worse misconception of Gladstone than the following?—"He had drawn up so many budgets that he was getting accustomed to the grosser side of life".[2] No one at the time suggested anything of the kind; the

[1] Selborne, *Memorials: Personal and Political*, 2nd series, vol. 1, p. 58.
[2] Stirling Taylor, *Seven Nineteenth Century Statesmen*.

man who could be blamed for "abstract reasoning" was never accused of being impractical. Indeed, taking 1866 as an example alone, "Time is on our side" shows both the reasoner and the wise practical statesman.

But there is a more serious defect still in modern criticism—the attempt to explain the problematical Gladstone by denying him altogether. It is rather amusing to find the contemporaries baffled and the twentieth-century writer at his ease. What Bagehot stressed as the chief difficulty about Gladstone, the author of *The Victorian Illusion* insists never existed at all. While contemporaries, statesmen in action and journalists with their entire critical faculties in play, reiterate that Gladstone's intellectual construction was abnormal and complicated, we hear that "Gladstone was the sublime ideal of the Victorian average".[1] And the Victorians received him not! "There is no reason to believe", Mr Dance continues, "that he ever conceived an original political idea, or adopted a policy which had not been suggested by somebody else." Who is immune from this devastating sentence? Mr Dance has ignored, if he had the sympathy to realise it, the courage of Mr Gladstone. If he carried out a policy that was inevitable, he was not seldom the only man who dared to lift his voice. If his simplification of the tariff system, his ardour for reform, his zeal to purify the life of Ireland, and his charity towards oppressed peoples were all reflections and echoes of the past (and to that extent unoriginal), who will not allow the appeal on his behalf? You cannot destroy the character of an English statesman by charging him with

[1] E. H. Dance, *The Victorian Illusion*, p. 27.

treading in the steps of the younger Pitt, accepting what Russell accepted, acting where Disraeli merely spoke and following the better part of Palmerston. He was, in many ways, the pioneer in courage if not in thought; and we cannot understand how so average and conventional a borrower could merit the suspicion and hatred of a great number of Englishmen. "Gladstone", we are further told, "always did what was expected—usually long after people had expected him to do it."[1] It is incredible that Palmerston could have been so obtuse in 1864 as to show surprise! These recent judgments, when placed side by side with the words of contemporaries, are worthless.[2]

In February, 1864, *Fraser's Magazine* included an extremely interesting article on "The Political Temper of the Nation", and the future of Gladstone was discussed with frankness. We have said that the difficulty of understanding him damaged his reputation and lowered his chance of being accepted as a leader.

"He combines the extreme of impressionableness with the extreme of want of intuition. Mr Gladstone's education renders him capable of diving into the depths of every problem, but it has not bestowed on him the faculty of judging the relative values of his discoveries. Such a man was not formed to be a leader. Leaders must never doubt. No politician can or does feel sure of Mr Gladstone. As an auxiliary he is incomparable. The necessities of his nature demand that he shall be guided by a will and a character stronger than his own—and where can such a man be found

[1] E. H. Dance, *The Victorian Illusion*, p. 28.
[2] Cf. the curiously uneven judgments of Gladstone in O. F. Christie, *The Transition from Aristocracy*, pp. 229–30.

on the Liberal side? One there was (Cornewall-Lewis) pre-eminent for simplicity, strength of intellect, depth and range of knowledge and firm judgment; but, alas, united England now bewails his untimely loss. Two contending rivals, the two impossibilities, as we might venture to call them, stand face to face."

"Such a one was not formed to be a leader." And yet, within five years, he had become a very great leader of men. Cobden and Bright believed this would happen. He had behind him the loyalty and devotion of the English working class, when it was at its full tide of wisdom and prosperity. To the professional politician a mystery, he was, while they were still plumbing the depths of it, accepted outside as the fearless and untiring champion of progress. He found his true place on the platforms of provincial halls though he never became a demagogue. To the people his message was unmistakable. They had begun to tell him to his face "that he was a tower of strength" before the ablest politicians (with the exception of Russell) imagined that he could ever lead. The real interest of the period lies in this; that the working classes measured what the statesmen and journalists deemed incalculable; and by so doing, altered not only Gladstone's position in English public life, but shifted too the political centre of gravity. The Second Reform Bill campaign determined, in the fullness of time, that the "tumult of debates" in Parliament would not "impede" or "disturb" the great social forces. But in the 'sixties their time had not yet come. Gladstone had to be judged, for the moment, by the politicians alone, and they found him unfathomable and unsearchable.

CHAPTER III

THE COMMERCIAL TREATY WITH FRANCE, 1859–1860. LETTERS FROM COBDEN TO GLADSTONE

"Bear in mind that my leverage here...has been my great promises in your name of large changes on our side."

Cobden to Gladstone, December 5th, 1859.

IN a periodical article already quoted, the attention of readers was drawn to the part played by Gladstone in the negotiations leading up to the Commercial Treaty with France. The purpose of the writer was to vindicate the "strong silence" of Palmerston in the early part of 1860, and to describe the policy of the Chancellor of the Exchequer while his master was apparently dumb. "Mr Gladstone's exultation knew no bounds; the premiership was almost yawning to receive him. With an excellent partner in the firm (Gladstone) and a capital traveller (Cobden) out of doors, there was every prospect of a roaring business being done."[1] The judgment of succeeding generations has been to condemn Palmerston and to support the partner and the bagman. The story has been well told in Morley's *Life of Cobden* and in Hobson's *Richard Cobden: the International Man*; but several letters from Cobden to Gladstone in the autumn of 1859, among the Gladstone Papers, make the picture more complete and give a lively account of Cobden's

[1] *Fraser's Magazine*, February, 1864.

early impressions in Paris. What is important from the point of view of Gladstone's career, is that the Treaty and the negotiations leading up to it gave him a reputation as a fighter and, through bringing him closer to Cobden, brought him closer to Bright. As Cobden said, writing to his friend, "I have told you before that Gladstone has shown much heart in this business. He has a strong aversion to the waste of money on our armaments. He has much more of our sympathies. He has more in common with you and me than any other man of his power in Britain"[1] (1860). Further, the temper in which Cobden faced his work was likely to appeal to Gladstone as a man even more than to Gladstone as Chancellor of the Exchequer. No language could be stronger in its appeal to him than that which described free trade as "God's diplomacy". After his first visit to Gladstone at Hawarden in September, 1859, we have a letter to Chevalier in the same strain, the sentiment being exactly that of M. Fould when the negotiations had begun.

"I see no other hope but in such a policy for any permanent improvements in the *political* relations of France and England. The people of the two nations must be brought into mutual dependence by the supply of each other's wants. There is no other way of counteracting the antagonism of language and race. It is God's own method of producing an entente cordiale, and no other plan is worth a farthing. I don't like the tendency of affairs on the continent. Every year witnesses a greater number of armed men, and a more active preparation in the improved means of human destruction.

[1] Morley, *Life of Cobden*, vol. II, p. 296.

Depend on it, this is not in harmony with the spirit of the age."[1]

It was with this attitude that Cobden began his great task. The first letter of the series dated August 5th, 1859, asks if he can come to Hawarden to talk over the matter. "My good friend M. Chevalier insists very pertinaciously [2] that the Emperor cannot reduce his duties unless you help him by a corresponding movement. How you are to do so and fulfil Lord Clarence Paget's promise to keep up fifty line-of-battle ships, I don't know*." Gladstone replied on September 7th that "the question of com- [3] mercial relations with France leads outwards to a wide field and I am very glad that it does so. I am afraid that when history comes to judge all that has been said and done in France about us, and in England about France during the present year, the verdict will not be very favourable to our country*". One more letter exists before Cobden arrived at the scene of action, Paris, on October 18th.

The commercial settlement, he insists, will be best achieved by a diplomatic act or commercial treaty.

"I have impressed on M. Chevalier both by letter and in [4] conversation that we have no necessity to seek for customers for our manufacturers, that we have quite as much demand for our products as we can supply, and that the main difficulty with our manufacturers, is how to procure the raw material and the labour to supply the wants of the markets already open to us. By the way on this point, I may mention a fact which was half an hour ago related to me by a friend from Rochdale, who says that there is not a mill in that borough

---

[1] Hobson, *Richard Cobden: the International Man*, pp. 244–5.

in which some part of the machinery is not idle owing to the want of hands." (October 11th, 1859.)

The main part of the series of letters covers conversations and conferences whose substance is very well known; but the detail and the minutiae can still bear enlargement. These letters reveal, as they do in several other important sets on other topics, the pressure that was being brought to bear on Gladstone. One question we have to ask ceaselessly is "Who was applying the spur?"

COBDEN *to* GLADSTONE

Paris.

Oct. 29th, 1859.

5 "When I saw Lord Palmerston, he said 'You will perhaps send a line from time to time to Mr Gladstone and Mr Gibson and let us know how the land lies'. I have thought it proper to write to *him* and have begged him to let you see the letter. It is impossible to exaggerate the ignorance in high quarters here upon fiscal and economical questions. The consequence is a terrible fear of the Protectionists, the only party banded together with money to subsidise supporters. The French tariff is in a worse mess than ours was in 1820, and where they are to find Deacon Humes, Huskissons and Peels to reform it, I can't imagine. I certainly have met none yet. One of the difficulties I find is the suspicion every body has that I seek some selfish object for England. Certainly I stand in a better position to remove this feeling than if I were an accredited representative. The only other category they will put me in, if I am not to be considered an interested agent is that I am a fanatic, to which I have no objection.... After M. Chevalier had had his interview with the Emperor and before I saw his majesty, he [Chevalier] came straight to me, and said that King Leopold had at Biarritz, when speaking to the Emperor about England's Free Trade policy, pooh-poohed our pre-

tensions to sincerity in the matter and instanced as a proof that fowling pieces which could be made in Liège 40% cheaper than in England, were not allowed to be imported by us—(is this true?). [You will see by the letter to Palmerston that the Emperor attaches great importance to the observance of secrecy.] Would you be good enough to let me know by return, through the ambassador's bag, the exact truth of the matter. People shrug their shoulders at our invasion panic and call it insanity. I am satisfied that the Emperor and his ministers are beyond almost anything besides, seeking for a good understanding with England and that the people of France, if we did not insult and worry them with our absurd accusations, would never think of harming us."

We know from other sources that during November, Cobden concentrated on the task of winning over the Emperor, whose opinion varied from week to week. "The Emperor had been pressing M. Fould as to the precise advantage that France would gain in imitating the policy of England...so dependent on her foreign trade, that she was constantly in a state of alarm at the prospect of war. France, on the other hand, could find herself involved in war with comparatively little inconvenience." ("This remark", says Cobden, "struck me as disclosing a secret instinct for a policy of war and isolation.")[1] On this question of Napoleon's good faith, Cobden wrote again to Gladstone on November 11th, 1859—the Emperor

"must prove, in the sight of Europe, his desire for improve- 6 ment. It is this alone that I am anxious about. I would not step across the streets just now to increase our trade for the mere sake of material gain. *We have about as much prosperity*

---

[1] Morley, *Life of Cobden*, vol. II, p. 239.

as we can bear.[1] But to improve the moral and political relations of France and England by bringing them into greater intercourse and increased commercial dependence, I would walk barefoot from Calais to Paris ".

Despite the illness which overtook him on November 17th, Cobden "carried on the endless argument with the ministers in his bedroom ".[2]

We have a glimpse of the battle in the next two letters which include technical references to alcoholic tests.

COBDEN *to* GLADSTONE

Paris.
November 21st, 1859.

7   "I have been laid up with a cold which I caught in the London fog and being naturally a little wheezy, if not asthmatical, it has settled into something like congestion of the lungs and I am a prisoner in the hands of the doctors. I have consequently seen nobody since my return [Cobden left Paris for London on November 3rd where during the week he had a conversation with Palmerston who spoke of reports of French orders for iron plating for ships of war—and was taken ill on the return journey], excepting Chevalier who tells me the Emperor is increasingly desirous of doing something, that he is impatient because M. Rouher, who has been up to his ears in reports and documents during the past week, has not a plan ready for him, that M. Rouher has pleaded the necessity of seeing me before he can take a final step. The consequence is that I have appointed to receive M. Fould and M. Rouher in my bedroom tomorrow. It is of course wholly a question of details and it is only when we come to the items of their tariff that one can form an idea of the views of the government. I am always of opinion, that to have the desired moral and political effect, *the French*

[1] This is strange reading at the present day.
[2] Morley, *Life of Cobden*, vol. II, p. 239.

measure must be a solid reality. Otherwise we had better not act in common. It would be considered a servile concession, and the Treaty might, by the gentlemen across the floor, be called the 'Gladstone capitulation'. Leave me to put on the screw, in the interests of the French people, for a bold reform."

COBDEN to GLADSTONE

Paris.
23rd November, 1859.

" I send by this messenger a short letter to Lord Palmerston 8 giving an account of my interview with M. Fould and M. Rouher. I have sent these *two* letters to Lord Palmerston, because I wished to interest him, knowing *your* heart was in the business. Besides, a man has a right to feel that the child he has to father is his own.... But what puzzles me here is the stealthy secrecy one meets with at every turn and the difficulty of trusting any one where nobody seems to be trusted. For instance, M. Walewski is expressly excluded from our secrets. M. Fould told me this. Only imagine Lord Palmerston telling a comparative stranger that he must not make a confidant of Lord John! M. Chevalier tells me that M. Rouher is so surrounded by spies and protectionists at the Bureau of Commerce that he comes to him [M. Chevalier] to ask him to go to the Bureau and inquire for reports etc., as for himself, which the President of the department dare not ask for lest his object should be suspected."

This state of affairs in French official circles during the winter is generally known, but perhaps no document reveals the confusion better than a letter of Cobden's to Gladstone on November 29th, 1859.

(Private and confidential)

" I do not see how matters could be made to march very 9 differently from their present course. M. Rouher has instructions from the Emperor to prepare a plan—not a small but a comprehensive plan. The French tariff is in a worse state than ours was in 1820. Think of the task with no one to help him and afraid even of his own clerks, and yet in a week to be told to produce a reformed tariff. The poor man is almost knocked up.... Now for a little incident to show you the state of mind of the people I am dealing with. A few days since, M. Chevalier on his daily call, pulled a droll face, and said that in a conversation he had just had with M. Rouher, the latter remarked, 'There will be a record preserved of our proceedings, a sort of historical record, in which the minutes of our negotiations will be kept, and I should like it to appear that we had not conceded all that Mr Cobden demanded, and that he should be made to yield more than he originally proposed'. I laughed outright and told my friend M. Chevalier that I was willing to be put in the most disadvantageous position as a diplomatist. M. Magne, the minister of Finance and M. Billault, the outré protectionist home minister are also ignorant of all that is contemplated. Now what a French minister values above all earthly, and I had almost said, all heavenly considerations, is his portfolio.... The fate of Sir Robert Peel is not encouraging for them, and it is impossible to talk to them without perceiving that they are in what schoolboys call a 'great funk'. The fear I always have is that some other diplomatic brewerage in hand, may swallow up my poor scheme. I remember meeting poor Porter[1] in Paris in 1840, when he thought he was about to obtain some commercial concessions from M. Thiers, but a grand diplomatic squabble about Syria blew all his fine plans into the air."

Though Cobden's labours came to a successful end, it is extremely interesting to note that there was some

[1] Cf. Cobden's Speeches: Manchester, July 4th, 1846: *Speeches*, p. 201.

justification for his fear of a miscarriage. The very week he was in London he tried to see the Foreign Secretary but failed. "I doubt whether Lord John is not just now attaching more value to the spirited turn of a phrase about Morocco, than to my efforts to lay down a commercial cable that shall bind these two great countries together."[1] Gladstone did not share this view. Writing to Mrs Gladstone about the negotiations (January 11th, 1860), he said "The measure is of immense importance and of no less nicety, and here it all depends on me. Lord John backs me most cordially",[2] and again "he was both a loyal colleague and a sincere friend to the budget and to the French Treaty".[3]

In December, 1859, the negotiations reached their most difficult stage, and Gladstone, by then, realised the full importance of the Treaty, not only to himself as Chancellor of the Exchequer but to Europe as a whole.

"For this panic [Napoleon's plan to annex Nice and Savoy] the treaty of commerce with France was the only sedative. It was in fact a counter irritant, and it aroused the sense of commercial interest to counteract the war passion. It was and is my opinion, that the choice lay between the Cobden treaty and not the certainty, but the high probability, of a war with France."[4]

He was learning his lesson well, but inclined to misgivings. Writing on December 2nd, 1859, Cobden can understand Gladstone's uncertainty about *recognised* negotiations,

[1] Morley, *Life of Cobden*, vol. II, p. 238.
[2] Morley, *Life of Gladstone*, vol. I, p. 655.
[3] *Ibid.* vol. I, p. 664.   [4] *Ibid.* vol. I, p. 657.

10 "involving your entire financial plans for next year and even years to come. I am and have been full of wholesome suspicions from the first, but unless the Emperor turns sharp round upon a month's eager solicitude for a Treaty and declares himself adverse [which is not his reputed way of doing things] to all that he has been professing since I have been here, the matter must go forward to a successful issue. If he should take such a course as you seem to fear, I should be almost inclined to join a rifle corps myself! [But bear in mind this has all happened since October 25th.] We ought not to be too impatient if they require a week more before a tangible proposal can be laid before you. I will ask you for a week and no more."

We know, from Morley, the strain under which Gladstone nearly collapsed; it was his impatience as Chancellor of the Exchequer that Cobden was trying to restrain. In concluding the letter, Cobden says that he cannot interview Rouher at his bureau for fear of the clerks, but protests that he was forcing the pace. "I took the opportunity of intimating to M. Rouher, through M. Chevalier that it was necessary, with a view to your arrangements, that the basis of the Treaty should be accepted within a week." The letter (December 2nd, 1859) ends on a favourite though curious theme, the good faith of the Emperor.

Replying on the same day (December 2nd, 1859), Gladstone made no secret of the difficulties at home.

11   "My dear Mr Cobden," he wrote, "Your letter considerably reassures me, but the truth is that I stand in the middle between two lively apprehensions. The disposition nay determination of the English people or of that portion of them who choose the House of Commons to have a bound-

less expenditure, of itself both creates a real difficulty about commercial reductions (fruitful as they are after but a short interval) and also engenders a lethargy and indifference very unfavourable to the efforts necessary for overcoming it. This lies on one side and on the other the knowledge that Louis Napoleon has formidable obstacles to face, that he must be governed in the main by his political interests, that he has to choose between the éclat of the treaty *plus* the gratitude of certain classes immediately benefited (for I do not suppose the general benefit is as yet believed in) and the hostility of other classes thinking themselves injured. Finally (however Gallican) I cannot feel the fullest confidence in the truth-fulness of those with whom you are dealing till we have something to hold them by. This, I fear, confidential communications also being unofficial would hardly supply. Were the year 1860 an ordinary year with us, I should care little, but it is a very extraordinary one in many respects. If it is to pass (bearing in mind the lapse of the annuities) without anything done for trade and other matters, it will be a great discredit and a great calamity, and it will I fear postpone the hope of measures in that cause almost indefinitely."

On December 5th, 1859, Cobden reminds Gladstone that he received his real mandate at Hawarden. "Pray 12 bear in mind that my leverage here, from the first, has been my great promises in your name of large changes on our side*." In the last letters of this series, we have an additional proof of the conviction among the negotiators that the scheme begun in the name of commerce must be pursued in the interests of European peace.

Paris.
12th *December*, 1859.
"Saturday last was according to M. Rouher's promise 13 through M. Chevalier, to have brought me a counter proposal

29

from the former gentleman, but up to this moment it is not finished. But I cannot say I feel very great confidence. I will not at all events run the risk of misleading you. It seems to me probable that when M. Rouher presents a report with thirty or forty pages of reasons for the alterations recommended, the Emperor may naturally require time to consider them, and that it will therefore be impossible to fix a day or perhaps even a week when the business will be ripe for your hands. I am very sorry that you are every day being pushed into a financial corner. I wish it was August instead of December for there is no doubt that ultimate good will come from protracted discussions of these economical questions so new to everybody here. Today for the first time since I returned to Paris, I have seen Lord Cowley and had a long conversation with him. He tells me that when he was at Compiègne nothing could exceed the eagerness of the Emperor for a commercial treaty. He spoke of it as a matter on which he was quite decided. But since his return from London, Lord Cowley says he perceives a change, and that now the Emperor talks of the great difficulties in the way. This morning Lord Cowley called on M. Fould and had some talk on the subject with him and he corroborates what M. Chevalier had told me, that M. Fould is very earnest in the matter on *political grounds*. In fact, M. Chevalier told me that M. Fould considers it the only way of averting war with England. M. Rouher shares his opinions and although they are aware that they must face a great protectionist outcry, yet both M. Fould and M. Rouher seem, from political considerations, to have entered heartily into the advocacy of Free Trade. (Entre nous) In the course of the conversation with Lord Cowley, he said he had received a letter from Lord Palmerston who in speaking of the Treaty observed that he was not anxious for it unless we got as much from the French as we gave."

There can be no doubt that Fould was converted not so

much by economic reasons as by preoccupation with the uneasy and hostile state of feeling in England against France. We have here, too, further testimony to Cobden's anxiety in December; Napoleon could have wrecked the scheme. He was still the major obstacle when Cobden wrote on January 7th, 1860, to Gladstone, "It is possible that the Emperor may think *we* attach so much importance to the Treaty, that he can make it a bribe to make us agree to something else".[1]

Finally, Cobden urged that the Commercial Treaty alone could "allay the warlike excitement in England", and the letters are important for our purpose because they furnished the arguments which Gladstone used in Parliament on February 10th, 1860.

COBDEN *to* GLADSTONE

December 16th, 1859.

"...May it not be necessary for you to consider the 14 propriety of bringing on your budget earlier than March? Might it not be well to mention the Treaty in the Queen's Speech and bring on your budget a week after the meeting of Parliament? Would not this be advisable with the view of allaying the warlike excitement in England? There can be no doubt that the fact of a large measure of commercial reform extending over the next five years having been determined upon by the French Emperor, will, when known, do much to change the feeling in England towards him. In the North of England especially, where Free Trade is made a Test Question, the effect of a really sound measure will be quite magical. In the midst of all this warlike din, which is every day costing so much to England, the announcement of

[1] Morley, *Life of Cobden*, vol. II, p. 248.

a commercial treaty with France would operate like a flag of truce between two hostile camps."

Gladstone replied on December 17th, "I do not indeed anticipate quite so great an effect on public feeling as you do".

COBDEN *to* GLADSTONE

December 23rd, 1859.

15 "The Emperor is said to prepossess in his favour every one who has more than one audience with him. I will not confess too much, but there is certainly something attractive in his simple and natural manners. If he have any affectation it is in a certain tone of humility (young ambition's ladder) in his language and gestures.... We are laying down a cable to hold the two nations together. I entreat you not to suffer any avoidable delay to take place. On every ground, the argument for despatch is irresistible."

The Commercial Treaty with France was the basis of the great budget of 1860, one of the most critical events in Gladstone's career. While Cobden was in Paris writing regularly to the minister he was doing something far more important than making a report. The direction of Gladstone's future steps became apparent, the character of his friends determined. A struggle with Palmerston, a new position in the party, a reputation in the country for Liberal and even Radical sympathies, an alliance with the men who tore to shreds the old arguments of foreign policy, lay before him inevitably. The first phase approached—the battle with the Lords. But for the time being, the sponsor of the Treaty found himself in the middle of study of alcoholic percentages lifted above the grosser details. He spoke now of "nations" as he was afterwards to speak of "our own flesh and blood"; the vocabulary changed at the first step on the new highway. In the House of Commons, on February 10th, 1860; he said

"If you desire to knit together in amity those two great nations whose conflicts have often shaken the world, undo for your purpose that which your fathers did for their purpose, and pursue with equal intelligence an end that is more beneficial. Sir, there was once a time when close relations of amity were established between the Government of England and France. It was in the reign of the later Stuarts.... But that, Sir, was not an union of the nations; it was an union of the Governments. This is not to be an union of the Governments, it is to be an union of the nations."[1]

So, as on many subsequent occasions, he found, amid statistics and clauses, a new principle. Though men accused him of being the servant of a capricious intellect, he now obeyed the promptings of a noble heart. Here, for the first time, he proclaimed his new allegiance. "Gladstone is really almost the only cabinet minister of five years' standing who is not afraid to let his heart guide his head a little at times."[2] By the autumn and winter of 1859, Gladstone had already realised that his relations with the old Whigs were beset with difficulties. Cobden more than anyone else had helped to make the issue clear. And it was to Cobden that Gladstone turned in the New Year, with the confession that he felt isolated from his colleagues.

[1] Bassett, *Gladstone's Speeches*, p. 277.
[2] Cobden to Bright. Morley, *Life of Cobden*, vol. II, p. 237.

THE COMMERCIAL TREATY WITH FRANCE

January 14th, 1860.

16   " I cannot refuse my concurrence to what you say with respect to the present state of things.."...Previously "the very first prompting of inward instinct (had been) to seek advice from persons in the same situation of the same habits of mind and political training and connections. It has been a great happiness of my public life (to do this)....But at the present moment for the first time it fails me, I mean within the narrow circle of those who are equally with myself aware of the course of affairs. Gross extravagance constitutes a public danger. Men who ought to have been breasting and stemming the tide have become captains-general of the alarmists. On the other hand, I sorrowfully admit that for the moment the whole country is possessed."

CHAPTER IV

THE BUDGET OF 1860: THE STRUGGLE FOR ECONOMY IN THE CABINET AND IN PARLIAMENT. REPEAL OF THE PAPER DUTY: ARMAMENTS

"We are in a period of great interest and hope.... To promote 17 this operation (the Commercial Treaty) has been for the last few weeks I may almost say the operation for which I have been living. I have seen in it...the consummation of the Tariff Reforms begun in 1842."

Gladstone to Sir James Graham, January 16th, 1860.

"We live in anti-reforming times. I sometimes reflect how 18 much less liberal as to domestic policy in any true sense of the word is this government than was Sir Robert Peel's and how much the tone of ultra-toryism prevails among a large portion of the Liberal party."

Gladstone to Sir James Graham, November 27th, 1860.

SCARCELY had the broad outlines of the Commercial Treaty been fixed, when Gladstone became involved in what was, on his own confession, one of the sternest battles of his career. He wished to repeal the Paper Duties; and instantly found himself face to face with the Lords. He was fighting for economy; and the Cabinet was bent on increasing armaments to protect the country from a French invasion. These two obstacles, which would have forced any ordinary Chancellor of the Exchequer to resign, were entangled. The documents printed by Mr Guedalla[1] prove that the invasion

[1] *Gladstone and Palmerston* (the Palmerston Papers), 1851–65, edited by Philip Guedalla (1928).

bogey occupied ministers' minds while they were dis-
cussing how to fight the Lords; and perhaps the plan
of Morley's narrative at this point tends to give the
impression that there were two distinct battles, and that
one succeeded the other (it must, in fairness, be stated
that Morley quotes Sidney Herbert's views on the state
of Europe in 1859). There was one common element in
the double struggle, and that was the attitude of Palmerston. On the Lords' question, he cancelled the effect of
Gladstone's speeches in the House; and on the armaments question he was frankly unregenerate. Some
letters among the Gladstone Papers show how Bright
held up Gladstone's arms in 1861, when the struggle
became intense. Throughout, also, there can be no doubt
that Gladstone had a herculean task in the Cabinet; as
time went on, his only loyal colleague, Gibson, was swept
along with the tide of panic and scare. In both 1860 and
1861 resignation and defeat were familiar words. If
Gladstone could describe his position in these words
(over the Paper Duty), "General policy, justice to
particular interests and the positive obligation of Treaty
form in this case the threefold which it is proverbially
so difficult to break" (July 20th, 1860, to Palmerston),[1]
it would be true to say that the Chancellor of the
Exchequer found an equally obstructive "threefold
cord" across his path; the opposition of the Lords, the
unsympathetic attitude of Palmerston, and the warlike
temper of the country. We prefer, therefore, to regard
the struggle with the Upper House, and the struggle
with a powerful phobia, as two phases of one tremendous

[1] Guedalla, *Gladstone and Palmerston*, p. 144.

struggle. They were, indeed, continually present together in Palmerston's mind:

"I see that some question is to be asked of you today as to remission of taxes in lieu of the Paper Duties; but in the present state of affairs and with the accounts we have received of the determination of the Chinese Government who seem to say *je veux qu'on me batte*, any repeal of any tax or any reduction of any tax seem for the moment to be wholly impossible" (to Gladstone, June 1st, 1860).[1]

This was Palmerston's temper; and Gladstone, no less, fought a double-headed monster during the two years. At the beginning of 1860, Gladstone's greatest problem was how to reduce taxation when faced with a certain and large increase of expenditure—largely due to armaments and their application. The cost of the China war ("a new paper weight" *Punch* called the bill of 4 millions), and the expensive construction of iron ships of war, had both to be covered. But he persisted in his policy of simplifying the scheme of customs duties, keeping on some small charges alone. Morley tells us that some economists regarded these as "a blot on his escutcheon",[2] and we have an interesting letter of Bright's to the same purpose, though of a later date.

Rochdale.
April 11th, 1862.
"Dear Mr Gladstone,   19

I enclose a letter on your proposed private brewing license. It is from a cooper and I think he has reason in his complaint. [The letter is in the form of a petition addressed to Bright— occupying three closely written foolscap sheets, from a cooper

[1] Guedalla, *Gladstone and Palmerston*, p. 135.
[2] Morley, *Life of Gladstone*, vol. 1, p. 659.

in Melton Mowbray. The fact that it was addressed to Bright
is eloquent in itself.] I am surprised that you should consent
to the imposition of these small, annoying and unproductive
taxes. Mr Bass tells me the question of doing justice to the
brewers is of no consequence. They can brew so much
cheaper than the private brewers, that the 3*d*. a barrel is not
worth a thought, and I am quite sure this must be so. I think
your proposition is a retrograde one, and should not have
come from you, and I shall say so when the House meets.
I suspect a very little pressure would induce you to surrender
this small Tax; small but unpleasant, and more like the Taxes
of a past time than of our day.

> Always very truly yours,
>
> J. BRIGHT."

Gladstone introduced his great budget on February
10th, 1860, undergoing a severe physical strain. But the
effort not only enhanced his reputation in the Commons;
it made him, for the moment, the most conspicuous man
in England.[1] Deputations by the score waited upon him.
While he frightened his own party ("We don't know
where he is leading us"), he was hailed as a champion
by the Radicals. Northcote said, "No doubt Mr Bright
would be delighted by the expedient of reducing expenditure on defences, and a reformed House of
Commons elected under his exciting eloquence would
be delighted too, and would enjoy taxing property".[2]

---

[1] "I confess I find it difficult to write and congratulate you on
your whole budget. I could really almost have wept over it. The
enormous expenditure for armaments coming from the same
government which proposed the Treaty is an offence against
common sense." From Cobden, Feb. 25th, 1860 (Gladstone
Papers).

[2] Lang, *Sir Stafford Northcote*, p. 101.

In the middle of the excitement Russell introduced a Reform Bill, although Gladstone did his utmost ("I will go down on my knees") to dissuade him. It was abortive from the reform point of view, but it did fatal mischief. It delayed Gladstone at an important moment; it arrested "the tail of the financial measure". By the time Russell withdrew it, Italian Affairs, the China War and the scare of a French invasion, occupied the public mind to the full, and obscured the earnest purpose of Gladstone. Near the end of May, the action of the Lords in rejecting the bill affecting the paper duties, had forced one conclusion on Palmerston's mind. Whatever happened, there must be no talk of resignations. (Memorandum of Gladstone, May 26th, 1860): "Lord Palmerston's (letter) came in sum to this: that the vote of the Lords would not be a party vote, that as to the thing done it was right that we could not help ourselves, that we should simply acquiesce, and no minister ought to resign".[1] From most of these propositions Gladstone emphatically dissented. But there was a danger that Palmerston's view about resignation would not be followed. On July 6th, he and Gladstone spoke so much at variance in the House, that the situation was deemed impossible. The speech of Gladstone once more aroused the enthusiasm of the Radicals, particularly when he denounced the "gigantic innovation on the constitution". Bright had no doubt what the Chancellor's next step should be. He wrote a letter on August 16th, which Morley has only quoted in part.[2] It contains a phrase

[1] Morley, *Life of Gladstone*, vol. I, p. 666.
[2] *Ibid.* p. 668 note.

which sums up admirably the spirit of Gladstone's finance, as well as dealing with the question of the moment.

Rochdale.
August 16th, 1860.

20   "...With regard to the Dog Tax, I have told Mr Young that I am rather in favour of spending less, than of discovering the means of collecting more.

I see the Lords are not slow at exercising their new powers and I am persuaded the course taken this session by your chief, and at his bidding by the House of Commons is one which will excite them to an improper and it may be, to a dangerous activity. I incline to think that the true course for Lord John, yourself and Mr Gibson, and for any others who agreed with you, was to have resigned, rather than continue a government which could commit so great a sin against the representative branch of our constitution. I fear we shall all look back on the past or passing session with regret if not with shame. I have a note from Mr Cobden this morning; he thinks he shall be detained in Paris till October; and that he may go to Egypt for the winter. Excuse my troubling you and believe me,

Yours very faithfully,
J. BRIGHT."

Despite Palmerston's attempt to rally the Cabinet, two ministers found their position exceedingly delicate. He, too, as we know now, had been crossing swords with Gladstone on other matters. "You won't pitch it into the Lords" was only a part of the disagreement. As we have said, many problems of expenditure were inextricably confused. For instance, before the Cabinet discussions in May, Palmerston had been enlarging on a subject which became an obsession as the months went by:

"I hope the elastic progress of the Revenue will enable us to find the £150,000 that Sidney Herbert wants.... I do not like the aspect of European Affairs; it looks as if we should have a disagreeable summer... a tolerable stock of elements of uncertainty" (April 12th, 1860).[1] A week later, he tried to make a breach in the Gladstonian defences on another topic, but this time he was repulsed. "The truth is that for many reasons there would be great advantage in putting that repeal (the Paper Duties) off altogether till next year when we shall have a rather formidable deficit to encounter"[2] (to Gladstone, April 20th). Gladstone asked in reply, "how could we recede when we have got the equivalent in the shape of the full Income Tax? Would not this seem to stand in the light of a fraud upon Parliament?"[2] It seems natural in these circumstances that there were threats of resignation. Long before July—after the withdrawal of Russell's Reform Bill, Northcote writing to his wife, had said, "It is difficult to believe in Gladstone's assenting to the large expense which is to be incurred for fortifications and the Chinese War, and I shall not be in the least surprised if he and Milner Gibson go out".[3] With the "threefold cord" of opposition, expensive armaments, the Premier's recommendation that the paper duty repeal should be postponed and his disinclination to fight the Lords, Gladstone's position was well-nigh intolerable;

---

[1] Guedalla, *Gladstone and Palmerston*, p. 131.
[2] *Ibid*. p. 132.
[3] Lang, *Sir Stafford Northcote*, p. 103.

but his sense of public duty strengthened his resolve to remain. "My dear Canning: I thought two days ago that we were breaking up. Gladstone talked at the Cabinet of the necessity of a substitute; and Johnny told me that if Gladstone went, he should take an early opportunity of following him. On Saturday's cabinet, however,... Gladstone talked over future plans of finance."[1]

The change of attitude was partly due to Cobden, for he wrote in strong terms against resignation on July 8th, 1860.

COBDEN *to* GLADSTONE (*from Paris*)

21 "...a looker-on at a distance upon what is passing in the House may suggest points for consideration which in the thick of the strife may not have occurred to you. All I would wish to suggest is that you do not take any step which involves the probability of your withdrawal from the government without taking into consideration all the circumstances in which you find yourself placed. The constitutional question, as between Lords and Commons is only one of these circumstances—nor is it the one for the settlement of which you are peculiarly responsible. Nay, with all deference, let me add that it is a question which will take care of itself without your special intervention. Be assured that a little discussion in the streets and in the daily penny press (of which there are 250,000 copies circulating daily in the United Kingdom against 70,000 of the high priced journals of which *The Times* claims between 40 and 50,000) will bring the privilege question to this conclusion: The House of Peers exists only on condition that it says aye to everything which the House of Commons does in matters of taxation and finance. Their vote was levelled

---

[1] From Granville, June 11th, 1860. Fitzmaurice, *Life of Granville*, vol. I, p. 381.

at you and your policy undoubtedly, but it would be playing the enemy's game to allow them, if you can possibly help it, to detach you from the other members of the Government on the privilege question. The country will in due time do justice to those who are assailing you personally.

But if you secede from the Cabinet and destroy the ministry, you risk the great measures of the session—especially the Treaty—which in their incomplete form will fall into the hands of our opponents.... It is hard enough, I confess, for me to seek an audience whilst everything in England breathes defiance and preparation for war—the Queen acting the part of Elizabeth at Tilbury fort with no Armada threatening her shores. Do not, I entreat you, allow yourself to be goaded into a withdrawal from your present post by the personal attacks of your unscrupulous opponents."

The confusion therefore proceeded; Palmerston fearing nothing but defeat. He was still intent on obstructing "the tail" of the financial measure—throughout July the constant refrain was, "Keep the paper duties on for the time being". Gladstone had no illusions about Palmerston's real reason; on July 24th, he addressed a remonstrance to the Prime Minister.

"I thought that the question had been finally decided by the Cabinet about bringing on the Paper Duty and I confess that I could not defend a recession from an intention we have so long and so repeatedly announced.... I must not write on this subject without confessing to you that I do not know how to reconcile the terms of your resolution on fortifications, moved last night."[1]

Palmerston replied

"It is quite true that the Cabinet, against my advice, came to the decision to go on with your paper duty of customs bill,

[1] Guedalla, *Gladstone and Palmerston*, p. 146.

but I conceive that this does not preclude me or any other member of the Cabinet from representing difficulties and dangers which the reports of our House of Commons Staff officers may lead him foresee as threatening that course. These authorities all tell me...that they consider defeat as nearly certain"[1] (July 24th).

The Cabinet was in truth "a mosaic in solution"; but Granville could again write to Lord Canning on July 26th:

"The Government continues as a whole. Gladstone has been on half-cock of resignation for nearly two months. He swallowed the constitutional question and a compromise was made about the fortifications. With great want of tact, having swallowed the last camel, he could not get over the gnat of being in the House when Palmerston proposed the scheme. Palmerston has tried him hard once or twice by speeches and Cabinet minutes, and says that the only way to deal with him is to bully him a little, and Palmerston appears to be in the right".[2]

This was the summary of the situation in August, 1860; in the following year the great question of expenditure on armaments remained insistent; the constitutional issue was met by the plan of including the various financial proposals of the year in a single bill, so that the Lords must either reject or accept the whole of them.

In 1861 the scare of a French invasion became a serious matter in politics. It is difficult for us to believe now that some of the language of fear and anxiety could have been used. [For instance, Palmerston writing about

---

[1] Guedalla, *Gladstone and Palmerston*, p. 147.
[2] Fitzmaurice, *Life of Granville*, vol. I, p. 386.

fortifications to Gladstone said, "Most things begun and left imperfectly finished are in some respects worse than if they had never been begun, but works of defence are peculiarly so, because they are liable to be taken by an enemy and to be turned against those whom they are meant to defend "[1] (July 24th).] Veritable midsummer madness! Bright's attitude to the French was a lesson and an example not only to the country, but to many ministers; and Gladstone agreed with him. But the ear of mankind was deaf to the wiser counsel. Even in 1859, Sidney Herbert had been fearful of danger; Gladstone retorted that to increase the estimates to provide defences would be "a betrayal of my public duty". One of his letters in 1860 shows how he clung to his purpose:

"The weak point is the fortification plan. I do not now speak of its own merits or demerits, but I speak of it in relation to the budget. It is a vile precedent to give away money by remission and borrow to supply the void and in the full and chief responsibility for having established this precedent I am involved not by the budget of February but by the consent of July to the scheme which involved the borrowing" (September 3rd, 1860).[2]

In January, 1861, he received two letters from Bright to which he replied, before the climax of the struggle came. The first, of January 1st, 1861, clearly explains its own purpose; it is intended as a shield and buckler for Gladstone in the hour of trial at Cabinet discussions. No plea for economy and a jealous watching of the estimates could have been more timely. One eloquent

[1] Guedalla, *Gladstone and Palmerston*, p. 148.
[2] Morley, *Life of Gladstone*, Appendix, vol. II, p. 816.

passage, that which contains a prophecy about Gladstone, deserves to rank with the finest estimates of him ever written.

Private.   *Rochdale.*
                                        January 1st, 1861.

22 "Dear Mr Gladstone,

I have received the inclosed copy of an address which I understand is likely to be signed by a considerable number of members on our side of the House, and which is afterwards to be presented to Lord Palmerston. I have had nothing to do with it in any way, and it is probable, that for reasons which I need not now explain, I shall not sign it. It has originated, if I am not mistaken, with some persons in the City of London acting along with some members of the House who are strong supporters of the Whig party and very friendly to the Prime Minister. I think the address judicious in every way, and I hope it may receive many signatures and produce some result. I have been requested to take care that this copy does not 'get astray and into wrong hands', and in sending it to you in *confidence*, I believe I am not departing from this injunction.

I send it to you that you may know what is going on, and that you may be armed the more fully for the discussions which must almost immediately arise in the Cabinet. The reasons for a large reduction of Estimates are many—but the strongest with some ministers are to be found in the expressed will of their usual supporters, and therefore I conclude that the knowledge that this address has been signed and presented, will tend to make some of your colleagues more willing to listen to reason than they have heretofore been. I feel convinced that the maintenance of the existing rate of expenditure—will not long be possible. In this country there has been great prosperity for two years past—but now there is a change evidently approaching. There has been and is now going on, an enormous increase of building for spinning and manufacturing purposes, whilst the prospects of a supply of cotton and of a sufficient demand for yarns and cloth are becoming rapidly less cheerful.

The crisis in the U.S. *may have* a tremendous influence on this country, and any great check to trade here is felt over the whole country and will affect the revenue. The wretched harvest, too, is telling upon us, and the uncertainty in which the future of Europe is felt to be, chiefly owing to the Question of Venice, operates unfavourably upon men's minds and disinclines them to transactions extending over considerable periods of time.

And now when you have escaped from the China War, surely the 30,000 men or thereabouts, which have been employed in it, may be got rid of, unless indeed, as seems likely, Lord Elgin has succeeded in making peace impossible by this barbarous destruction of the Emperor's palace. Depend upon it, peace must ever be insecure so long as you have armed ships and armed men always ready for attack, prowling about parts of the globe many thousands of miles away from the immediate control of the Government, and from those who pay taxes to support them. This China business has evidently very few friends in the country. Most men feel that it cannot be defended, and many feel that it is a grievous stain upon the character of the nation. I think therefore you may protest very strongly against the policy which has led, and leads to such results, and that the friends of economy in the Government, have now the power to *coerce*, by force of argument, their colleagues into a more rational course.

The men whose minds are full of the traditions of the last century, your *chief* and your *foreign minister*, will still cling to the past, and will seek to model the present upon it,—but the past is well nigh really past, and a new policy and a wiser and a higher morality are sighed for by the best of our people, and there is a prevalent feeling that *you* are destined to guide that wiser policy and to teach that higher morality.

...I have had no letter from Cobden since he got to Algiers. 'I hear that he was sitting at an open window eating strawberries when last seen.'

...I forgot to tell you when I came back from Paris, that he and everybody in France, and I suppose everybody in England too, are wishing you to give up the first stage in the alcoholic test as applied to the customs duties on wine—in Paris this test is discovered to be a positive though unintentional departure from the meaning of the Treaty, and most injurious to the French Wine Trade.

I am hoping you may have the courage and the success which often waits on courage, to cut off so much of your estimates, as to enable you to set free our friends the paper makers and at the same time to do what is now possible to restore the position and powers of the House of Commons in matters of Taxation. I am quite sure that the Towns and our great populations will regard the government with increased favour if they see them having some regard to the pressure of taxes upon them, and now when the China War is over, and when there exists no cause for suspicion against our friends across the Channel, I think you have an opportunity of preventing a discontent which will certainly arise if a contrary course be taken.

I did not intend to do more than to say a few words about the inclosed address when I began to write. I must ask your excuse for this long letter, and for intruding thus upon your time.

I am, Yours very truly,
J. BRIGHT."

Gladstone's reply on January 3rd breathes sincere gratitude for the timely help "in making colleagues more ready to listen to reason".

Hawarden.
January 3rd, 1861.

Private.

"Dear Mr Bright,   23

Your enclosure and the account you give of it have afforded me the highest pleasure. It is the very thing I could have longed for, and it is admirably timed. At the same time you will readily guess that it is in about 5 *weeks* the Estimates must be on the table in all their details for the Army and Navy, and as it is also intended to put forward the Civil Estimates and present them as early as possible this year, *there is not a moment* to lose. I speak literally.

At the same time I hope that all the men of weight and likelihood at least will have the opportunity of signing it. In ordinary circumstances, the opposition ought to keep down expense. Now they stimulate it. I know of no Engine likely to be effective for good at this time except such an address as the present.

I suppose the organisation of the 'Committee room No. II' party may have been thought of: even if rusty. You probably did not mean to suggest my taking any part in the proceedings, nor would it I think be right. But on the other hand I am desirous to know whether I may make use of the paper with any of my Colleagues and to what extent there. At present I confine myself to informing them that I have been informed some steps are being taken among the supporters of Government on behalf of reduction in the public expenditure.

This is certainly an important epoch in our system of expenditure. I look upon the present scale of it as an enormous evil, and I wish heartily well to measures for its due reduction, whatever may be their possible results in the sense of party politics.

I must reserve until we meet the subject of the alcoholic test: but I cannot postpone until that time the duty of thanking you for being disposed to believe that I desire the adoption of a policy, of which the temper shall not be likely to produce more wars in China. I believe and have long and often urged, that along with the temper of our Foreign policy under a series of Governments, there is occasion to think much more upon our system of Naval Armaments all over the Globe. I expect to be in London about the 15th, but I hope to have the pleasure of hearing from you here.

I confess that as yet I have seen but very few signs of an anxiety for thrift. I am glad you find them more abundant.

Believe me,

Very faithfully yours,

W. E. GLADSTONE."

Within a week, Bright had written again. This letter of January 9th is one of considerable importance.

In view of the letters which Palmerston wrote to Gladstone in February, Bright proved himself to be completely right in thinking that the critical question was that of French and English naval armaments. He shared with Cobden, and with Gladstone, the belief that an understanding with France could be achieved by the exercise of tact and patience. He did not know that there were few "sensible men" in the Government who would be prepared to take the line of peace instead of suspicion. His concluding reference to the state of affairs in America showed his foresight; he was to be one of the few in the coming civil war who would be on the right side. And no less his words on India, a subject on which he was admitted to be a great authority, reveal the sure grasp and the piercing eye. He was grappling with tradition in two of its most hidebound forms—foreign and imperial policy.

50

Rochdale.
January 9th, 1861.
"Dear Mr Gladstone,   **24**

I do not see any harm in your making such use as you may think judicious of the address I sent you. I never saw it, or even heard of it, till it was sent me in the shape in which I sent it on to you.

I learn now that from 50 to 60 names are likely to be attached to it. Some members refuse, not wishing to declare themselves supporters of Lord Palmerston—some say that they dislike any *private* proceedings—some that they think the Government will see the propriety of making reductions etc., but scarcely any I think are of opinion that the present expenditure ought to be or can be continued. I have given an opinion that the address with 50 names will be useful, and have suggested that no time should be lost in sending it in.

Some members have insisted upon it, that no good will be done till some arrangement is made with France as to naval armaments. This might easily be done if the difficulty on this side the Channel were no greater than that on the other side. I am convinced that Mr Cobden could arrange the matter with the Emperor in one-tenth the time he spent on the commercial treaty, if he knew he would be heartily and honestly supported by the English Court and Government.

I do not see why yourself and Mr Gibson, and other sensible men in the Government should not propound such a scheme to your colleagues—the arguments for it are conclusive—and there is nothing but danger ahead in your present course. Only this year, what has been done? The Treaty, and the abolition of passports; and Mr Cobden now tells me he has obtained the consent of the French Post Office to an increase of the weight of letters through the French Post, and he has written to Rowland Hill, to urge him at once to have the arrangement concluded. More—much more may be done. I believe there has *never before, in any time*, been a Government in France more willing to act honourably and amicably with England, and that anything we can reasonably ask will be conceded. At least £15 millions a year might be saved to the two countries at once, by such an arrangement as I speak of, besides the increasing peril of war from these frightful preparations and this incessant military excitement.

The recent news from the U.S. is causing great anxiety in this country. Our dependence upon the South for our Cotton is a very unsafe position to be in. This year, the crop is likely to fall short of our needs, and with so much excitement there, and such confusion, political and monetary, I have great fears for the future. This year will be very unlike the last in this country and I look for much difficulty and much suffering in many branches of trade.

The Question of India, too, is not looking better. Since the Revolt, I cannot see that *one single thing* has been done to show that we have learned anything. An expenditure of 45 millions! We so govern that country as to spend more than 6 millions more than the utmost we can squeeze out of it by the utmost pressure of the screw of taxation and seem only more hopelessly involved than ever. Your India Secretary here, and your Governor General there, are fair weather statesmen only—'the services' in India, and the old tradition are altogether too strong for them. They want an 'iron hand' upon them such as Cromwell once calmed the anarchy of England with.

But, you will say, I am writing beyond your department,—not wholly so, seeing that Indian finance can never again be entirely severed from that of England. England expends this year £76. millions, and India spends £45. millions—in all 121 millions sterling! Is it not enough to justify the utmost punishment which can befall our ruling class? There are no institutions in this country or in India worth this price, and some day the People will say so, and will act upon that opinion.

Believe me, very truly yours,

J. BRIGHT."

Gladstone admitted in his reply that no part of the letter could be denied; and he couples Disraeli's name with that of Bright on the question of armaments. It was not the last time that these two men, so different in temper and outlook, would be together on the unpopular side.

Private.　　　　　　　　　　　　11, *Downing Street.*
　　　　　　　　　　　　　　　　January 15*th*, 1861.

"Dear Mr Bright,　　　　　　　　　　　　　　　　25

I see the address to Lord Palmerston is criticised in the public press, but if strongly signed it will do good.

Your plan for an understanding with France as to the reduction of Armaments is, I think, in principle sound, and it is also, I think, supported by a good deal of authority. Something that looked like it was once spoken by Sir Robert Peel. It is said that Lord Cowley deems it practicable, Mr Disraeli has urged it in the House of Commons. I shall be well pleased indeed to see an opening for any practical measure in this sense. And it is recommended at this time by the fact that the Emperor of the French has (besides bearing a good deal from us) been behaving in the most friendly manner towards us. On the other hand his conduct in Italy, which I can call (at Gaeta in particular) nothing less than shameful, puts a plea into the mouth of those who represent him as determined upon keeping Europe in hot water, and as impracticable therefore for a purpose so delicate and difficult of execution as that of which we now speak. I feel this to be a real and serious difficulty with reference to your suggestion at the present moment, desirable as it is in itself, and appropriate as it may justly be held to a series of amicable proceedings on the part of France towards England.

> I remain,
>
> Very faithfully yours,
>
> W. E. GLADSTONE."

In the next three months, Gladstone had to face the full storm of the panic party; their spokesman was Palmerston, and he spoke incessantly of the danger from France. Once more Gladstone found himself in an insupportable position; only the desire to see his financial hopes come to fruition kept him in the ministry—this explains not only his replies to Palmerston but also his letter of April 15th, 1861, to Bright. No Chancellor of the Exchequer ever gave a more signal proof of devotion to his office than did Gladstone during these months. We quote two of Palmerston's letters as examples. "No doubt a full Exchequer is a good foundation for national defence, but if the superstructure is wanting, the foundation would be of small avail and if the French had the command of the sea they would soon find means to make a full exchequer empty." Then follows a wonderful specimen of an evergreen argument which has caused infinite misery to mankind. "Our measures of defensive preparation may doubtless make the French angry, but only because they render us secure against the effects of French anger" (February 25th).[1] Gladstone's answer to this reveals a weariness that might have been expected months before. He feels

"the unseemliness of renewing during the present session

---

[1] Guedalla, *Gladstone and Palmerston*, p. 160.

a series of struggles such as were those of last year upon the Fortifications, the Paper Duty and the Question of Taxing Bills.... The most natural sequel to what I have said would be at once to place my resignation in your hands. But one strong public motive, over and above many which are personal, disinclines me to any such step at the present juncture. I earnestly desire, and I feel it to be a duty unless it is crossed by some duty yet more imperative, to render my account of the measures of last year...this account can only be rendered in full by means of the budget, which in proposing measures for the future, will also wind up the past.... I desire to be in at the death, even though it should be my own"[1] (February 26th, 1861).

The end of the long struggle was fast approaching, and Gladstone's supreme concern remained the Budget, even though his chief declared that he did "not intend to make the fate of my administration depend upon the decision which Parliament may come to upon your proposal" (April 14th, 1861). Everything must be secondary to the work of redeeming the pledges of 1860. Gladstone did not wish the controversy with the Lords to be reopened, or the wisdom of the machinery by which they were to be checkmated questioned. He wrote to Bright on April 15th, asking for his complete forbearance on this point. Personal feelings, even the zeal of a Radical, must be set aside in the grand effort to get the Budget through:

Most private.   *Downing Street.*
                             April 15th, 1861.

"My Dear Mr Bright,   26

     I hardly know whether there is any other subject or

---

[1] Guedalla, *Gladstone and Palmerston*, p. 161.

occasion on which I should be justified in making a request of you, but I venture it now and I think it is one you will readily grant.

It is our intention to adopt a mode of procedure in regard to financial measures this year, which among other advantages, will materially tend to prevent a recurrence by the Lords to the great operation of 1860. But I most earnestly hope that nothing will be said today which can put upon it an invidious construction. I would indeed hope more than this; namely that, if we do what is right and effectual, we should all through say the very least possible about it. All however that I venture to ask for today is that you will use your influence, and if need be give an example, in favour of treating this part of the subject today with an absolute forbearance, and of taking time to consider how it should be handled hereafter. Of course I mean on the supposition that no provocation from the opposite side shall compel a different mode of proceeding.

W. E. GLADSTONE."

After the Reform Bill of 1866, there is no more important event in this transition period of Gladstone's life, than his struggle to repeal the Paper Duties and his jealous watchfulness of growing expenditure. In no uncertain way "he wound up the past" and prepared for the future. His activities brought him into closer touch with the Radical demand for the overthrow of a traditional foreign policy. In every particular he proved the panicmongers to be wrong. The fortifications were never required. As a result of his labours, increasing expenditure on the army and navy was checked. The repeal of the Paper Duties created a weapon for the working class. As he himself said in 1865: The measure "called into vivid, energetic, permanent and successful action the cheap press of this country. To the most numerous classes of the community it was like a new light, a new epoch in life, when they found that the information upon public affairs... came to them morning after morning, gave them a new interest in the affairs of their country, and with a new interest in these affairs, a new attachment to its institutions ".

And he might have added, a new channel between himself and " the most numerous classes of the community ". Within three years, he was to raise his standard on their behalf; but he provided them first with the means of following, judging and understanding public affairs. In a sense, he was educating his masters before acknowledging them, and not afterwards as Lowe argued.

These were the great benefits of Gladstone's financial policy, and it carried him far along the Liberal path. But the most abiding impression left on the mind is the eminence of its author. In a session which left "sore places in the mind " he gave a supreme demonstration of his high sense of public duty, his moral courage, and his devotion to the most exacting office in the Cabinet. There has never been a Chancellor of the Exchequer who guarded more grimly the public finances. Everything he endeavoured to maintain, every innovation he resisted, every principle he supported, make up a policy which posterity must endorse. In finance, as in so many things, it has been abundantly proved that "time was on his side ".

NOTE TO CHAPTER IV: GLADSTONE'S ESTIMATE OF 1859-1860

We have Gladstone's estimate and summary of many critical parliamentary sessions through the length of his career, in the Gleanings, Diary, periodical articles and so on. To this collection, the following letters dealing with the years 1859 and 1860 are an interesting addition:

GLADSTONE *to* COBDEN

December 2nd, 1861.

27   "I do not dissent from what I take to be your main proposition with regard to recent expenditure. But I am sorry to add that I think the country has exacted it, though I admit that in demanding such a scale of outlay it has had a balance of encouragement from the Government. I doubt if Lord Derby's Government would have spent less—the Liberal party would certainly if in opposition have breathed a more wholesome air so far as expenditure is concerned. The main point in which I think the existence of the present Government has been beneficial is the Italian Question. It is true that English opinion is now favourable to Italy, but it was not so three years ago and we may have done something in assisting the change."

GLADSTONE *to* COBDEN

December 13th, 1861.

28   "Lastly, I think it true that if in June, 1859, I had been able to foresee the amount of panic that was to seize the country and of expenditure and of danger that it would entail and the persons, some of them most pacific in temperament by whom it would be shared and fostered, I should not have been justified in accepting my present post, nor I think

tempted to accept it. But I did not foresee the very critical position in which I was to stand. At the same time, though I dread the continuance of efforts to which I feel myself unequal, yet looking at the whole case, as it has been and as it might have been, looking first and foremost at the one great witnessing act which you have enabled us to effect, I am glad that the future was hid from my eyes."

CHAPTER V

COBDEN'S INFLUENCE ON GLADSTONE: LETTERS, 1860–1863

"There are signs of reaction especially in the provincial press of England and the country will back you."

Cobden to Gladstone, July 2nd, 1860.

"COBDEN disturbs your tranquillity; he forces you to think and keeps you thinking, now with him, now against him."[1] Much has been written about the general influence of Cobden and it has been work well worth doing. The story of Cobden's life is still fascinating reading because it was largely spent in controversy. No man ever packed more facts into letters or speeches and at the same time made them more readable. Wherever we encounter Cobden, whether in Paris negotiating the Commercial Treaty or criticising ministers over a China War or attacking *The Times*, we find a formidable man. Like Samuel Butler in literature, he strove in politics "to irritate thought out of its inertness and convention and credulity", and his letters are full of those "little poisonous microbes of thought (and fact) which the cells of the world would not know what to do with". Perhaps the final judgment of the historian will be that Cobden's political knowledge was much greater than his influence and that, as Butler said of himself,

[1] W. H. Dawson, *Richard Cobden and Foreign Policy*, Introduction, p. 8.

60

"He was allowed to call his countrymen lifelong self-deceivers to their faces and they said it was quite true, but that it did not matter". With the larger problems of Cobden's influence we have here, however, no immediate concern. Our present purpose is to show that he set out "to disturb Gladstone's tranquillity". The seven letters I have printed in this chapter make it quite clear that he had arrived at a definite and characteristic conclusion on Gladstone's position in Palmerston's Cabinet. He seems to have thought that Whig foreign policy and expenditure would hasten a social revolution. He spoke so often on the impending upheaval that some sympathy can be felt on Delane's side in the controversy over redistribution of land which is fully dealt with in Morley's *Life of Cobden*. In particular, he warned Gladstone that he was in peril of being "labelled for life" by the policy of his colleagues. In July, 1860, as we have seen, he advised Gladstone not to resign, but in January, 1862, he wrote "separate yourself I entreat you from your chief". His opinion of Lord Palmerston has never been a secret and these letters can add nothing to our knowledge on that score. What they do prove is this. Cobden made it his business constantly to remind Gladstone that he had no permanent home among the Whigs, and that the country looked to him to break away from them. On the whole, it may be said that he spoke to a willing listener. In addition to Gladstone's own difficulties in the Cabinet and with the Prime Minister in particular, came this insistent voice from outside, confirming his suspicions and strengthening his resolution.

In the first three letters of this series, he pours more

scorn on the invasion panic, and then ends on a note of warning.

COBDEN *to* GLADSTONE

January 12th, 1860.

29 "The reliable accounts I get are that in the dockyards of France there is no general activity.[1] The report from Toulon is 'there is next to nothing doing'. Officers of the English Army from Jersey who have gone to Cherbourg give a similar account. It is true the English people have gone mad; that they have been the willing victims of as great a hoax as any in our history, not excepting that of Titus Oates. But I blame those in high places, who knowing better or who ought to know better, still lend themselves to the delusion.... The occurrence of a couple of bad harvests and a dearth of cotton and one or two other events that I could name, would turn the whole country against this expenditure and against the responsible authors of it. I am astonished that the governing class in England play so shortsighted a game. Have not most of them sons and successors?"

COBDEN *to* GLADSTONE

January 23rd, 1860.

30 "...a larger fleet than we had at the height of the great war in 1809. Depend on it there will be a revolt sooner or later if you and your party have nothing better to announce as a corollary to the Treaty than this state of things. I don't of course expect any sudden revolution in your policy or expenditure, but in my humble opinion the announcement of the hope or intention of a better state of things ought to accompany the announcement of the terms of the Treaty in the House."

[1] The case against Cobden's view appears in a letter of Lord John Russell: Morley, *Life of Cobden*, vol. II, p. 371 note.

LETTERS 1860–1863

January 29th, 1860.

"The torrent of prejudice, passion and hatred is not 31 turned back upon itself in a day. But a reaction is certain to come and recollect that Mr Disraeli has put himself in the position to act upon it, for you will remember his qualified allusion to the possibility of entering into an arrangement with the French Government for reducing mutually the armaments of the two countries. He can fall back at any time on that declaration. If any good, politically or morally is to flow from this Treaty of Commerce it must lead to an abatement of our naval armaments. I will never rest from my labours to put down so revolting a state of things as is implied in the present armed attitude of two neighbouring nations.... For example, I will assume that I should succeed in obtaining the signatures of the leading bankers, merchants and manufacturers of England and France to a declaration in favour of an understanding between the two governments for putting a limit to the waste of capital involved in their immense naval establishments. Would not such a proceeding compel the attention of their respective rulers?... Though I am illiberal enough to suspect that such a proposal would be less acceptable to our governing class than to any government in Europe, yet with such a qualified or conditional offer of mutual reduction of armaments from the Emperor's Government, I could become a very troublesome person in the evenly balanced state of political parties at home."

The fourth letter contains a remarkable prophecy. Suppose Napoleon III adopted the tactics of Palmerston and "played the revolutionary game in Europe". What would be the effect of this policy on Liberalism in England? Napoleon did try to play this game in the next six years, but Cobden did not foresee either that it would come to nothing, or that "the so-called Liberal party in the House would be a good deal more Palmerstonian than he realised". Writing to Gladstone on July 2nd, 1860, Cobden said that each morning press notices about France were collected in the office of the Minister of the Interior. The English notices were usually very insulting.

32   "The only circumstances which could drive Napoleon to desperation would be to find the Government showing by its acts the same hostility and mistrust towards him which are exhibited in the journals. Has it never occurred to Lord John and the wiser heads of our aristocracy that it would be in Louis Napoleon's power to play the revolutionary game (which Lord Palmerston and Lord John adopt for the moment in South Italy) on a much larger scale to throw all Europe into a state of commotion by declaring himself an ally of the Poles, the Hungarians, the Venetians, the Christians in Turkey and even of the 'nationality' of Germany as against its tormenting governmental divisions? Imagine an appeal from Kossuth and the Hungarians...invoking the aid of the British democracy to prevent their own government from fighting the battle of their oppressors. I believe every one of these nationalities would gladly accept his aid. All this should be taken into account by a political party in England which aims at holding office by popular support....Seeing how the aristocratic chiefs of our present Government fraternise with Garibaldi to secure a cheer from the British Liberals, surely we must give Louis Napoleon credit for sagacity enough, if driven to extremities to play the same game in other countries....Every word of what I have written has, I confess, an allusion to the huge engineering job for new fortifications. For heaven's sake let us...put this mad scheme aside. There are signs of reaction especially in the provincial press of England and the country will back you. To adopt this project would be a gratuitous insult to France.

It would break in pieces the so-called Liberal Party in the House and destroy the Government."

In the last three letters Cobden warned Gladstone that his future would be mortgaged if he remained identified any longer with the foreign policy of Palmerston. In order, these letters deal with the American Civil War and with Gladstone's future:

COBDEN *to* GLADSTONE

December 11th, 1861.

"I entreat you not to allow yourself to be drawn step by 33 step into a position with reference to the American Question which your conscience does not wholly approve. I remember on two occasions meeting Lord Aberdeen at the Bishop of Oxford's near this place (Midhurst) when he declared to me, very emphatically and sorrowfully that he had been forced by the press into the rupture with Russia, which he pronounced 'the most useless and unnecessary war in all our history'. Can it be doubted that such a reflection troubled his conscience to the day of his death?...I trust.you will not allow yourself to be injuriously compromised by preparation for war which at the present moment cannot be justified. You have been a victim to this policy in reference to another country to an extent of which perhaps you are not aware.... After a very diligent study of Hansard and other sources of information for the last twenty years I have come to the deliberate conviction that your present chief has been the evil genius of this country in its relations with France and other countries...this evil genius seems now at seventy-seven to be bent on pursuing a similar policy towards America....I saw the leader in double-leaded type in the *Morning Post,* second edition of last Friday week, issued at the very hour when your Cabinet meeting was called to deliberate on the despatch to be sent to Washington. That article intended to go with the despatch by the steamer of the following day was almost of itself enough to prevent a peaceable solution of the difficulty. Though war may not arise, *you* will be thwarted and discredited by the expenditure —the unjustifiable expenditure which is to be incurred before an opportunity of an answer is given to the accused party. You are sending troops to Canada. Let me call your attention to a letter from the Duke of Wellington in 1814 addressed from Paris to Sir George Murray upon the subject of the war then going on between this country and the United States in which he said 'I have told the ministers repeatedly that a naval superiority on the Lakes is a sine qua non of success in a war on the frontier of Canada'....For the South and Slavery, if Christianity is to survive, there can be no future."

COBDEN *to* GLADSTONE

January 15*th*, 1862.

34 "We stand on such different grounds and our careers of action in public life must ever be so separate that I sometimes think it hardly fair to try to take a common view with you into the future. For myself I would never be tempted by any consideration to enter upon official life. When I see what cabinets sometimes do and with the tacit approval of a minority of conscientious men, I am almost inclined to add a verse to our litany and in addition to 'plague, pestilence and famine' to pray for deliverance from a seat in a cabinet. Yet I am free to confess the world cannot go on upon my theory, I admit that men must co-operate. But my object in troubling you is to say a word about your position with reference to the present Government. In the nature of things the ministry as at present organised cannot last long. I do not believe in its existence unless you save it and I don't think you can do so without a considerable reduction of expenditure. The policy of your chief has always been opposed to this. Now I have always had the impression that when your chief came

to make his political will, he would if he could make the Tories his residuary legatees. But what I am most anxious about is that he should not label you for life with an unexampled expenditure. I am quite sure if the Tories come in they will immediately throw themselves upon two issues, great reforms of the law and a large reduction of expenses. You may remember when we walked in the stubble field at Hawarden, talking about the Treaty which thanks to you alone in the Government was practically successful, I alluded to the significant speech made by Disraeli about an arrangement between France and England for a reduction of armaments. When I asked you whether his party would allow him to take that line if they were in office, your reply was 'that party will make great sacrifices for office'. What I am concerned about is lest you should find yourself some day leaving your post and giving over to your successors the immense advantage of making your extravagant budgets the starting point for a great reduction in Government expenditure. You have shown signals of distress whilst carrying the Treaty and the paper duty repeal, at the heavy burden of expenditure to which you were administering as finance minister.

Bear in mind that these financial questions will this year be discussed amid uneasy prospects of a gloomy state of trade. It is clear that apart from the American Civil War, there was a crisis impending at least in the cotton branch from over-trading and that a part of the prosperity on which you have been so freely drawing was fictitious.

What in a word I wish you to do is to avoid being placed in a situation in which you may by the accidental fall of the ministry be made responsible for the rest of your political life for the recent public expenditure as a normal state of finance. Separate yourself I entreat you from your chief rather than allow yourself against your better judgment to be placed in such a position."

67

COBDEN *to* GLADSTONE

December 19th, 1863.

35 "I consider that you alone have kept the party together so long by your great budgets. But I think it a cruel misfortune that you have been working for such a chief. You see I always talk treason in this way the moment I take my pen up to write to you."

It is interesting to speculate what kind of letters Gladstone would have received from Cobden had he lived longer. But he died in 1865. Many of the conclusions he drew in these letters were wrong, and "the reaction" that he felt so imminent came a good deal later. There was, in fact, "a dearth in cotton", but as Gladstone himself confessed later on, the conduct of the operatives during the crisis proved to be exemplary and no violent fate overtook "the aristocratic chiefs of the government" or their "sons and successors". Cobden misunderstood Lord Palmerston, and English sympathy with the Italians could not be compared for a moment with Napoleon III's vacillating policy towards the Poles. If Palmerston could get a cheer from British Liberals by playing the revolutionary game, Napoleon never mastered the moves.[1] And again, if Gladstone alone "had kept the party together by his budgets" up to 1863, he came perilously

[1] E.g., what would Cobden have made of the following? "Comme le moindre incident de nature à mécontenter les Italiens dans les difficultés auxquelles pourraient donner lieu les négociations de la paix suffirait pour prétexter une manifestation hostile à l'Empereur, je crois devoir dès aujourd'hui prier Votre Excellence de me permettre de m'abstenir de faire célébrer publiquement le 15 août la fête de Sa Majesté" (August 3rd, 1866). French Consul General at Milan to Drouyn de Lhuys. *Origines Diplomatiques de la Guerre de* 1870–1, vol. II, p. 365.

near breaking it up by his Reform Bill in 1866.[1] But, from the point of view of Gladstone's development, the mistaken forecasts in Cobden's letters are of minor importance. The great Radical had separated him from the mass of politicians, had fathomed his character and foretold his destiny. In substance, the letters said, "Do not be swept along with the tide", and in that sense Cobden exercised an important influence on Gladstone. Though he died before the Second Reform Bill struggle and the beginning of the stormy period in Irish affairs, the voice remained, both because it was "independent of dissolutions and even of the course of time" and because there were two Gracchi of Rochdale.

[1] *Diary of Mr Speaker Denison*, p. 201.

CHAPTER VI

THE MOVEMENT FOR PARLIAMENTARY REFORM, 1860–1864

"He'll shape his old course in a country new."

WE take the question of extension of the franchise to be the most important one in Gladstone's progress towards avowed Liberalism, not because an interest in reform must be looked upon as a "Liberal qualification". The object of the search has been to discover which forces determined Gladstone's future, promoting him, as it were, from mere Cabinet rank to the position of a popular leader. We are looking for an altered dimension; and it is in the question of reform that we find the explanation of increased breadth. Other questions, particularly in the department of finance, had developed in him qualities absolutely vital in the responsible minister of a democratic state. But no question affected his outlook like Reform. It brought him into contact with the masses of his own countrymen for the first time; before, when these sympathies had been evoked, they had been at the service of that part of mankind we call foreigners. It also helped them to form an estimate of him which was irrevocable; the men of South Lancashire may have been as wrong in their sweeping judgment of him as the men of the Ionian islands when they hailed him as a liberator. He was, as he told Ruskin once, an out and out "inequalitarian";

and he felt no answering thrill when the professor from
the eminence of Hawarden Castle perversely turned his
eyes from the Cheshire plain to look on the colliery
chimneys of Buckley. It was as big a mistake for the
artisan to regard him as a democrat as for the statesman
to call him a disciple of Tom Paine. But the judgment
given could not be reversed. Once he had given serious
attention to the claim of the working men—that is, in his
case, once the matter had become a duty—his course was
altered. He became the spokesman in politics of the
middle class working men; they hailed him at once as
their greatest representative. The very language he
invariably used when speaking in or near Liverpool,
strengthened their conviction. He had been born, he
always said, in that great city which had seen so many
vast changes since his youth; changes produced by
infinite labour, by the development of commerce and
shipping. The affection for his birth-place came to be
very naturally confused with an enthusiasm for industrial enterprise and the artisan. We cannot help
feeling, both in justice to the man and to his followers,
that it was the greatness and width of his subject, rather
than its theme which inspired him on these occasions.
It was the type of eloquence that Burke employed over
the activities of the North American Colonists. Gladstone never became a demagogue or even a Radical.
Though from this time on, his greatest speeches were
delivered in the country, and though he relished the
appeal to vast multitudes, we repeat that it was not so
much his desire to make the popular appeal or to be
supported by the popular voice, but to execute his

operations on a grand scale. He remained the grave deliberator of Cabinets; nor did he discard the character of speech and analysis which gave him a unique place in Parliament. But after 1863, he found the desire to speak in the country irresistible; there he was in contact with forces. His very description of the people as "the great social forces" is a paradox. For it expressed both a great truth and a grave misapprehension.

There was considerable point in Lowe's celebrated comment: "If you want venality, if you want ignorance and facility for being intimidated...where do you go, to the top or to the bottom?"

There was an opportunity, though no one and least of all Gladstone took it, to parody the phrase and ask, "If you want blind prejudice, if you want self-interest and fear of change, where do you go?" It is necessary to say this, because much was said in Parliament in 1866 about "fitness" and "qualification" which was grossly misunderstood outside, which was undoubtedly true, and which challenged every principle of representation. Did Gladstone associate himself out and out with the interests of the working man? His very language proves that he was blind to some of the essential weaknesses of the class. He saw the "might" and "the majesty": a revelation which never vouchsafed itself to the more worldly, more hardened and more disillusioned Robert Lowe. Beaconsfield caught a glimpse of the vision; no nineteenth-century statesman of the first rank was denied it, and perhaps in our time, only Wilson experienced it. This is what we mean by describing Gladstone's phrase as one containing great truth. "A people's voice." It was the most fruitful period of democracy. There was a width, a largeness of outlook in popular causes which the world but rarely sees nowadays. For the time, there was a majesty in the people. They were a great tribunal and there were great causes before them in the next two decades. We catch, in Gladstone's utterances, a different note from that of Bright's. He too was misrepresented as the voice of a class—the nature of his profession and his fear of the "residuum" are enough to refute the charge. The difference lay here. Bright did much, if not the bulk of the pioneer work in the country on behalf of reform; and of necessity, the work "vulgarised" and destroyed any romantic or idealistic theory about the working class. He wanted to give them power, because he was convinced that the rulers of the country chronically misgoverned. They were to be ferrets in the warren of unnecessary and expensive wars, reactionary and ill-matured policy. Gladstone took up the work when the demand existed, and so he had different thoughts and employed different language. Under Bright, the working man claimed a right; under Gladstone, he was invited to share a privilege. Character and circumstances made Gladstone's call to the people far different from anything that had been heard before. Lofty, disinterested, inspiring, the character of the appeal revealed the man who had come late on the scene, and who transformed an agitation into a noble expression of principles. In many ways, Gladstone did for English politics what John Wesley did for English religion. Both set out to satisfy the crying need of a people; neither wished to give more authority to the people than they deserved. Their standard was raised, but they were still to be governed by the old methods.

Reform, then, settled the direction of Gladstone's footsteps; and the parliamentary battle over reform in 1866–7 was the cardinal event in Gladstone's career. It is necessary therefore in these years to discover the relation of politicians with the country on this subject, and like the physicist to show which way the forces were pulling. The first important question is, how far did the country wish for reform before 1866?

(i) *The Reform Organisations*

Mr Dance has said that the politicians "had no business to be bothering about parliamentary reform at all, since as the Earl of Shaftesbury said, nobody wanted it".[1] After studying the situation in England after 1859, we can only say that Mr Dance and his distinguished authority are both wrong. There was an intense desire, on the contrary, in almost every big town in England and in every important trade for an extension of the franchise. It has been left to an American to give us the first full and authoritative proof of this. The book, admirably documented, and based on an exhaustive examination of newspapers and trade-union reports, examines the whole position.[2] The thesis of the book is to disprove the assertion that there was an "absence of political interest and activity" among the working class during the 'sixties. If the book has made its point, it destroys once and for all, the charge, frequently heard in

[1] E. H. Dance, *The Victorian Illusion*, p. 33.
[2] F. E. Gillespie, *Labor and Politics in England*, 1850–1867.

1866, that Liberal ministers created an artificial interest in reform. "You cannot stop" said Lowe "when once you set the ball rolling." "Any demand for reform" says Mr Dance[1] "which existed in the country at the end of 1866, had been artificially created by the Liberals themselves in the course of that same year." The pith of the question is: "Can we prove that what Gladstone and Russell were accused of creating in 1866 was there already, and had been for some years?"

It is true that in 1860, "labour was yet too weak to have many spokesmen of its own. If the workers were to be incorporated in the body of voters, it meant that they had to enter into political relations with other classes and groups. The argument has been generally accepted that this very absorption of the working class in their attempts to work out their redemption along economic lines did in fact render them passive in political matters".[2] "A belief in the suffrage as a right" throughout this period has been ignored.[3] Spokesmen were lacking, and there was therefore very little to hear. But there was a keen interest in political affairs. When compared with the agitators of 1832 and 1842, the working men of 1860 were inarticulate. But "there is a volume of evidence as to the part taken in politics by men who had not even the right to direct participation. Therein a notable amount of interest and thought can be argued". Going back to the aftermath of Chartism, 1848 seemed to be "an opportune moment for the radicals", when the great

---

[1] E. H. Dance, *The Victorian Illusion*, p. 41.
[2] Gillespie, *Introduction*.
[3] Gillespie, *Introduction*, p. 12.

parties appeared to be in a state of disunion. Various reform associations were formed: e.g. "The National Parliamentary and Financial Reform Association" of 1849; and the old type of agitator—Holyoake is a good example—persisted. But these unions had their faces turned towards the past; there was still a suspicion of the middle-class leader, a man of Bright's type for example. One of the greatest changes which took place during the next ten years was the union of the working and middle classes in their demand for reform. Even in 1866 many politicians were not aware of this progress. Lowe mournfully declared that working class M.P.s could enter the House of Commons. Gladstone paid a tribute to the fusion in one of his speeches in 1866, but it had been accomplished years before. While Cobden could say in Manchester in 1849, that it would be impossible to induce the Manchester Free Traders to join a movement for democratic reform, two years later in the same place a great change had taken place.

"For I will tell you, the result of my observations and experience is this: that of all the rich men in the country, the most liberal men are those that you have among you in these two counties. It is not to be expected that a man who has a large balance at his bankers, and perhaps £100,000 Capital in his business, should rush at every proposal for change quite as readily as a man who is not so fortunately situated; because the natural selfish instinct occurs to him—'What have I to gain by change? I have got the suffrage; I don't want political power; I don't want the protection of the ballot'; and, therefore, you must make allowances for all such men; but, also, you must value them the more when you catch them. And I can assure you, if you go to Lombard Street, or any other quarter where rich men are to be seen, you will find much fewer Liberal politicians, fewer men that will ever join together, pulling shoulder to shoulder, with the working classes for great political reforms, than in Lancashire and Yorkshire; and I was glad to find, this morning, the hearty concurrence with which these men joined in advocating the ballot. Let it not be said by the great landowners, or any people elsewhere, that the Manufacturers and Millowners of this part of the world, those, at least, with whom I have ever been accustomed to associate, are afraid of giving to the working classes political power, and ensuring them in the full exercise of that power. The experience of this morning has redounded to the honour of those men; and if the union which I perceive to have arisen between the working classes and a large portion of those who should be their natural leaders in these struggles be cemented and continued, nothing can prevent you, be assured, from obtaining those political rights which you seek."[1]

And again, "Don't let anybody persuade you, the working classes, for a moment, that you can carry out any great measure of political reform, unless you are united with a large section of the middle and capitalist classes". It was from Birmingham, however, and not Manchester that the real impetus came. If the workers were ready to unite, the masters, "though aiming to undermine the territorial aristocracy, hesitated to do it by the aid of a popular movement which might go too far" (Gillespie). The Manchester men for the time being held back, Bright revived the subject. Though he suffered defeat in 1857, that election was in many boroughs a reform question. How great was the prejudice even then

[1] Richard Cobden at Manchester, December 4th, 1851. *Speeches*, p. 561.

against the working-class organisation is clear from Holyoake's reminiscence. "In 1857, the idea of labour representation was inconceivable." (It is interesting to notice that Mill contributed towards his election expenses.) In 1860, the whole question was raised to a new level. The unions decided that their own particular demands were included in, and would be assisted by, the reform question. The titles of some of the new societies are illuminating. For instance, "The Reform Society of City Boot and Shoe Makers" sums up in a phrase the trend of working-class interest. Town life, as Mr Hammond has pointed out, was being made much more attractive and progressive at this period. What the municipality did not provide, the working men themselves made good. Public libraries sprang up all over England; and in Lancashire and Yorkshire especially, these years saw the foundation of working men's colleges and mechanics institutes. With increased facilities for reading, members of trade unions sank the specific grievances of a trade in the larger national question. "A union of unions" took place. "Political Action" became the new cry of the trade-union councils, and through their activity the "Manhood Suffrage and vote by Ballot Association" was formed. Further impetus was now to come from another and extraneous source. The Polish Revolution of 1863 gave a *raison d'être* to many mass meetings, but the subject was always reform. The men who were struggling with their masters in the iron trade in the years 1862 and 1863, met to discuss their political rights in England, out of sympathy with oppressed brothers on the continent. But the visit of

Garibaldi showed even more plainly that Englishmen expressed their feeling for nationalists abroad by being reformers at home. A mass meeting was held on Primrose Hill for the purpose of supporting the efforts of the Italian liberator. The outcome of the gathering was "The Reform League", and after it "The National Reform Union". There was scarcely an agenda paper, resolution, or pamphlet of any working men's club or meeting which did not give the premier position to the question of the reform of the franchise. To talk then in 1866, as though some novel idea was being brought before the people is absolutely untrue. Some words Gladstone himself used in 1864 have caused misunderstanding. Speaking on Baines's Bill for lowering the borough franchise in 1864, he said

"We are told that the working classes do not agitate for an extension of the franchise, but is it desirable that we should wait until they do agitate? In my opinion, agitation by the working classes upon any subject whatever is a thing not to be waited for, not to be made a condition previous to any Parliamentary movement, but on the contrary, it is a thing to be deprecated, and if possible, anticipated and prevented by wise and provident measures...we must not allege the absence of agitation on the part of the working class as a sufficient reason why the Parliament of England and the public mind of England should be indisposed to entertain the discussion of this question".[1]

When a deputation from a trade union waited on him in 1863 it said, "If there had been any suspicion or disinclination towards it (i.e. confidence in the government) on the part of the working classes, it was due to

[1] May 11th, 1864.

the dissatisfaction with Parliament as to suffrage ".[1] He inquired about "the alleged indifference and apparent inaction of the working classes as to suffrage". They replied:

"Since the abolition of the corn laws, we have given up political agitation; (it is important to understand what this really means and what Morley did not point out—political agitation of the chartist or corn law type: the interest and the demand existed now in the union meeting) we felt we might place confidence in Parliament; instead of political action, we tried to spend our evenings in the improvement of our minds".

It was this very process of "improving the mind " which gave the working-class movement its strength and its tenacity. We shall have cause to deal in another place with the reasons why it interested and captured Gladstone. Here, the theory we wish to overthrow is the theory of an artificial ("ministerial" Lowe called it) agitation created in 1865. After Gladstone's speech on March 20th, 1866, *The Times* said, "There is no applause, not even an echo. We have listened in vain for the faintest note of approval, or the contrary, or bare recognition from the provinces". Delane spoke too soon. Within a fortnight, resolutions of approval had been passed at great meetings in Manchester (National Reform Union), Birmingham, Edinburgh, Leeds, Rochdale and Liverpool. Mr Dance would hardly dare to assert that Gladstone and Russell could have administered so much stimulant in so short a period. The truth is that the supreme and dominant interest of the working

---

[1] Morley, *Life of Gladstone*, vol. I, p. 759.

class between 1860 and 1866, was the question of reform. Gladstone described the position as it was in 1865 with complete honesty and truthfulness, speaking at Ormskirk on December 19th, 1867. "The attitude of the people was one of calm and tranquil expectation." It is right to dwell on this last word. The position reminds us of the Oriental tale, where the men were concealed in great jars waiting for the word of command "It is time". But for the stern parliamentary battle, there is some reason to believe that the working men would have been as grossly betrayed as were the forty thieves. But when the moment came, it was seized. And it could not so thoroughly have been used, unless every man had been in his place prepared. That preparation had been going on since 1860.

(ii) *The Influence of Bright between 1860 and 1865*

In considering the forces working upon Gladstone at this time, one question has definitely to be settled. We know that he passed through some novel experiences, and that after his speech of 1864 he was never the same man again. But we are at pains to show that there was nothing in this development which was in the nature of a capitulation; that he did not come to terms with any man or any body of principles. It was natural, however, for some of his contemporaries to brand a transformation of opinion as a surrender. The charge took one common form, and was that he "had taken the great mass of his supporters and laid them at the feet of the honourable member for Birmingham". One thing appears absolutely certain, from a study of the period, and that is Gladstone reached his conclusions without any prompting. He delivered a crushing reply to the accusation that he had become a pupil of Bright, in the House of Commons on April 26th, 1866; looking over the years from 1860 to 1865, there is nothing to detract from that statement. John Bright was in close touch with Gladstone between 1859 and 1861; when the Chancellor was fighting for economy and when Bright gave all his powers to the business of overthrowing a traditional foreign policy. He was in even closer touch with Gladstone after the Reform Bill was introduced in 1866; in some ways it would be true to describe him as applying the spur. But in the interim he exercised little influence over Gladstone. We have some expressions of Bright which show that he watched the members of "the Peace Party" in the Whig Cabinet with great anxiety. On February 5th, 1861, when Russell abandoned reform, he wrote, "I shall keep no terms with this government for the future. It is base—how long Mr Gladstone and Gibson will go through the mire with them, I know not". A letter quoted above shows his lively concern over Gladstone's future; it would be fatal if he followed the policy of the old parliamentary hands. The next time he came actively into contact with ministers was when the names for the Cabinet were under discussion in 1865. There, a letter of Gladstone's to Russell disposes of the idea that Bright had been forcing the ministry's hand, and of the suggestion that he should be admitted to office in a reform Cabinet.

"With reference to your remark about Bright," he wrote on December 11th, "he has for many years held language of a studious moderation about reform. And there is something odious in fighting shy of a man, so powerful in talent, of such undoubted integrity. Without feeling however, that he is permanently proscribed, I am under the impression that in the present critical state of feeling on your own side with respect to the franchise, his name would sink the Government and the bill together."[1] [The "remark about Bright" occurs in a letter from Russell on December 7th. "I have no objection to the message of Lowe, but I think Granville the best person to convey it. I no longer after Bright's last speech, consider him as hopeless. If we can get him to renounce his allegiance to President Johnson and to be a loyal subject of Queen Victoria, there are few better speakers in the House of Commons or any where else. But he must grow tamer than he is before he ceases to be the Wolf of politics" (Gladstone Papers).][2]

So far from exercising any influence, Bright had little in common with Gladstone in the intervening years. Even during the battle for economy when the friendship of the two men took solid form, Gladstone wrote to Palmerston at the end of April, 1862:

"In all good humour, I prefer not being classed with Mr Bright or even Mr Cobden: first, because I do not know their opinions with any precision—(two of Bright's letters in 1861 had, however, been pointed enough)—and secondly, because as far as I do know or can grasp them, they seem to contemplate fundamental changes in taxation which I disapprove in principle and believe also to be unattainable in practice, and reductions of establishment and expenditure for which I am not prepared to be responsible".[3]

[1] Morley, *Life of Gladstone*, vol. I, p. 790.
[2] Cf. also "I have not the slightest objection to be in the same cabinet with Bright, but I am sure his admission would upset the coach". Granville to Gladstone, December 7th, 1865.
[3] Morley, *Life of Gladstone*, vol. I, p. 683.

6-2

On the great question of the American Civil War, Bright definitely stood opposed to Gladstone's view. "The North would blunder through somehow", was Bright's conviction; and he described Gladstone's speech at Newcastle as "vile". At Birmingham on December 18th, 1862, he said:

"I do not blame any man here who thinks the cause of the North hopeless and the restoration of the Union impossible. It may be hopeless; the restoration may be impossible. You have the authority of the Chancellor of the Exchequer on that point. The Chancellor of the Exchequer, as a speaker, is not surpassed by any man in England, and he is a great statesman; he believes the cause of the North to be hopeless; that their enterprise cannot succeed. Well, he is quite welcome to that opinion... we are all equally at liberty to form our own opinion. But what I do blame is this. I blame men who are eager to admit into the family of nations a State which offers itself to us based upon a principle, I will undertake to say, more odious and more blasphemous than was ever heretofore dreamed of in Christian or Pagan, in civilised or in savage times".

This was a direct attack upon the Gladstonian salute to a new nation.

It is not true, therefore, that Gladstone had come under Bright's influence, when he introduced the Reform Bill in the House of Commons. No single individual indeed, but a close examination of the progress of the working class, had led him on to that position. He wrote in his Diary, October 14th, 1864, after delivering a series of speeches at Bolton, Liverpool and Manchester: "It is impossible not to love the people from whom such manifestations (i.e. of approval) come. Somewhat haunted by dreams of halls, and lines of people, and great assemblies. God knows I have not courted them". His reference to Bright when winding up the debate was equally emphatic; he had not courted or been courted by, Bright:

"Now, I come to another subject again of a personal character, and one with which the House has been made perhaps sufficiently familiar during our long discussion. I refer to my hon. friend the Member for Birmingham. It has been made a charge against the Government that they are identified with my hon. friend. It is admitted that we are the nominal Ministers of the Crown, but it is confidently or boldly declared that he is its irresponsible, yet its real adviser. To such a charge, couched in such terms, I shall make no reply whatever. Such persons as are disposed to admit it must have minds in a position entirely inaccessible, I will not say to deliberative reason or justice, but, at any rate, to any observations I can offer. In truth, such things are said, not to convince, nor to persuade, but if not to bewilder, at least to sting. But more specific charges have been made, and these it is right, that as Her Majesty's servants, we should notice. It has been stated that my hon. friend the Member for Birmingham has been the adviser of this Bill. On that subject, inasmuch as it raises an issue of facts, and is therefore one which admits of being dealt with, let us consider what has taken place. And I may preface my statement with this remark, that in my opinion, as well as in the opinion so gracefully, as well as manfully expressed by my hon. and learned friend the Member for Exeter, it would have been no disgrace to the Government, if policy had appeared to recommend it, that they should have consulted the great Organs of opinion in the different sections of their party with respect to the best method of framing a plan of Parliamentary Reform. Had that method been pursued, it would have been impossible to overlook—it would have been culpable if, through cowardice, they had refrained from consulting—my hon. friend the Member for Birmingham. But Her Majesty's Government felt no such necessity; and, as far as I am aware, did not in any manner or degree pursue that course of consultation. They did feel that, responsible as they had been for the formation and the introduction of previous Reform Bills, and being most of them, not wholly inexperienced in conducting the affairs of a Government, they had sufficient confidence in themselves, sufficient knowledge of the state of the public mind, and sufficient sense of their own responsibility to form their own opinion on the leading provisions fit to be embodied in a measure of Reform. We were, indeed, aware of the opinions of the hon. Member for Birmingham just as much, I believe, as, and no more, than the gentlemen opposite were aware of them. And I apprehend that we were aware of them through the same unfailing channels—namely, the public journals of the country. What we understood to be his opinions he stated in some speech delivered by him, I rather think at Rochdale, during the autumn, we conceived them to be as I will now state them, and my hon. friend himself will, I doubt not, have the kindness to correct me if I am wrong. There were, I think, four points principally put forward. Firstly, that there was a certain franchise which must be considered to be the maximum for counties, and that this was £10; secondly, that there was also a certain franchise which must be considered to be the maximum for boroughs, and that to make this satisfactory it should on no account be above £6; thirdly he considered that the extension of the franchise ought to be separated from the re-distribution of seats; and fourthly—he will forgive me if I do not quote him with sufficient precision—he thought that separation of the two subjects ought to take place in order that the interval of time between the two might mature and ripen the public mind after the passing of the franchise Bill, so as to obtain, if a later, yet a more full and conclusive settlement of the question. These, as far as my memory serves me, were the four points of opinion delivered by my hon. friend. And what have we done? We agreed with my hon. friend in one of them—we agreed with him in the policy of the separating the franchise from the re-distribution of seats. And should we not have been the most contemptible of all the poltroons ever misnamed Ministers, if, having that opinion, we had shrunk from acting on it because we might know well enough, without any gift of divination, that the leader, forsooth, of the Tory party would found on that circumstance a charge of subserviency which he himself knows to be thoroughly unfounded just as well as we do?"

Thus, in the opening of his great speech, Gladstone destroyed the charge that he had been acting under the influence of Bright. The very papers at the Museum are a silent witness to the truth. There is nothing of importance between 1861 and 1866; between criticisms of the minister over finance and over reform. Bright contributed absolutely nothing to the change. There was, it is true, an important sense in which Gladstone owed a great debt to Bright; he was the heir of Bright's labours. He saw the flaws, he altered the bias. Where the appeal had been made to a class, Gladstone widened and upraised it. "He extricated the vital or purely liberal elements from disintegrating Manchesterism." It was not until after Gladstone had become convinced of the justice of the popular demand that Bright began to write his letters "full of sugar plums". When the time arrived, he pressed the minister hard, but he never disturbed him while the leaven was working. The two men advanced different reasons for reform, and they were naturally separated in the time of staking their claims. When they had advanced to the common ground of action, or rather when the minister had caught up "the tribune" by another route, they became allies. But not before.

(iii) *The Series of Reform Bills: Gladstone and Palmerston*

One important phase remains in the story of Gladstone's relations with Palmerston; the correspondence and all that it implied following the famous declaration on Baines's Bill on May 11th, 1864. We think that a study of the documents disproves the Palmerstonian contention that Gladstone had said something dangerous. On two questions—ministerial agitation and the feeling of the country—Palmerston was definitely wrong. It is interesting to study his fluctuating opinions. On April 10th, 1854, he wrote to Russell, "I am not averse to improvement in our representative system...an attempt to make changes has the double disadvantage that on the one hand it is likely to create a resistance which must lead to an entire failure, while on the other hand success can only be obtained by a great and convulsive struggle". These were wise words for their time, but Palmerston had recanted ten years later. Between 1854 and 1860, as *Punch* said in a cartoon, "the cauldron would not boil"; and Russell's Bill of 1860 was a complete failure. At this hour, Palmerston thought fit to warn Gladstone that a sweeping reduction could only cause hostility.

"It would be desirable that in your speech tonight you should not represent the six pound franchise as an indispensable condition of our reform bill because it has become sufficiently apparent that the Bill will not pass into law with that Franchise in it. From all I hear I am led to think that if we were at liberty to announce the substitution of eight for six, and some increase of the county franchise our difficulties would disappear"[1] (May 3rd, 1860).

But the common feeling remained that the question was not urgent; *Fraser's Magazine* interpreted it to mean that the question was closed, though it mentioned one potentially sinister force. "We are witnessing the last stage of the period of reform. The building has been put into complete repair and men now are eager to be rid of the brick and mortar and to live in the fair mansion and to enjoy it." "England is now satisfied with her institutions." There existed, unfortunately, a dilemma between "finality" and the inclusion of men "whose moral and social worth gave them a title to the exercise of its duties".[2] Gladstone within three months shattered the hope that the hour was come when the house could be swept and garnished. His speech on May 11th raised a great controversy; and some of his own remarks afterwards, both in letters and in the edition of the speech, added complications. One thing, however, can be definitely said. The declaration "that every man who is not presumably incapacitated by some consideration of personal unfitness or of political danger, is morally entitled to come within the pale of the constitution" was not made on the *a priori* ground which satisfied Mill afterwards. Its basis was experimental; he had watched

[1] Guedalla, *Gladstone and Palmerston*, p. 133.
[2] "The Political Temper of the Nation", *Fraser's Magazine*, February, 1864.

the temper of the working class, examined thoroughly the question of "fitness" and declared himself satisfied. He could imagine no adequate defence of a system "that let in the lower stratum of the middle class and shut out the upper stratum of the working class". The Prime Minister, however, had seen nothing of the experimental work; he only saw the results, and these he vigorously challenged. It is necessary to examine very carefully what Gladstone actually said, in the light of the correspondence that ensued. In the advertisement to the edition of the speech he wrote: "Objection has been taken and even alarm expressed with respect to the breadth of the particular statement now in question. If indeed I am asked whether it was a deliberate and studied announcement, I reply that it was *not*; it was drawn forth on the moment by a course of argument from the opponents of the measure". Palmerston found many things in the speech for which Gladstone looked in vain. It is important, therefore, to take the debate as a whole, and then leave the smoke of controversy to clear itself.

The debate on Mr Baines's motion deserves to be better known than it is, because it gives a very full account of the progress of the working classes since the 'thirties, and because it is singularly free from the technicalities which the subject usually demanded. It was a political scientists' debate. Baines's speech, a model of fairness, ordered facts and restraint approached the subject in a suppliant manner. "I have to plead the cause of those who neither in person nor by representatives are present among us; to plead before an aristocratic jury for plebeian clients."[1] The grievance, he went on to say, which was felt by those for whom he pleaded, was that the great bulk of the Commons of England had no voice whatever in returning the Commons House of Parliament. His scheme went deeper than Mr Locke King's; his observation of the temper of the masses and the fact that the Palmerston administration was now stricken in years, forced him to the conclusion that the matter was urgent. "There is no time like a penultimate session for bringing in a reform bill." He discussed next one of the most vexed questions of that day; why were the masses so indifferent to the cause of Reform? If the need was so great, why did they not speak themselves? Mr Baines denied that there was no interest; indeed he had been spurred to this present effort by petitions from the National Reform Union at Manchester, and from the Working Men's Parliamentary Reform Association at Leeds. But he acknowledged "there have undoubtedly been causes which did tend in a certain degree, I will not say to create indifference, but rather to divert public attention from this great question". He argued that the very nature of the diversion increased the urgency. "It is morally impossible that they (the working classes) should long continue thus indifferent. Have not the people of England manifested sympathy on behalf of the liberties of the whole world?"—culminating in the "unparalleled reception to the great and heroic deliverer of Italy"..."I conceive it is totally impossible that those who value liberty so highly for others should be in-

[1] Hansard, vol. CLXXV, 3rd series, May 11th, 1864.

sensible to its value for themselves." Gladstone could have listened to no more compelling argument than this; it was a summary of his own development. But principle alone did not constitute the whole case of Baines; he had convincing evidence and he produced it. He described the growth of popular literature, paying a tribute to Gladstone's recent legislation as he did so, in the great towns. Men were interested in politics as they had never been before. A letter from Alderman Heywood of Manchester on the subject of popular progress and the cheap newspaper ended on a note of prophecy—to be fulfilled in 1866. "Should the present ministry be displaced and a conservative one called to the helm of affairs, the apathy of the people will no longer be a reproach to them; on the contrary a storm will be created of such intensity as will require a Reform Bill to subdue it." This was what Forster, an undoubted authority on industrial areas, meant when he said later on in the debate that a dangerous but covert feeling did exist. It is at this stage of the debate, when an amendment was moved by Mr Cave, that the arguments are of great interest to us, because they determined the trend of Gladstone's speech. Cave dissented, we think to a large measure rightly, from the suggestion that the working class had no representatives. The tendency of taxation, he said, had been to relieve their burdens, and their material welfare had able and constant representation. But he shifted to more questionable ground when he asserted that the working classes had shared the various warlike expressions of the country since 1860, and therefore took their place ungrudgingly in the great family of the nation. And again, using an argument employed by Lowe in 1866, why should the working man not wait for the suffrage until he ascended the social scale? Reward the frugal and the prosperous, and make the vote a coveted prize. "There is a perpetual recruiting from the working classes. When the heated air rises, the cold falls in constant circulation as in a well ventilated room." No argument more devoid of historical application could be imagined, as Gladstone pointed out immediately he rose; for it had never been considered in a previous reform of the constitution, and it struck, in effect, "against all extension of the franchise in the direction of the working class". The seconder of the amendment plunged still deeper into fallacies. Marsh taunted the proposer with the remark that the House heard much about the working class. "There was always a cheer when anything was said in their favour in the House." He revealed the gross inconsistency of the plea of working class indifference when he said that "great political and social reforms proceeded from the people". Let them speak first. "It was not the time when they did not ask." This was the weakest spot in the opposition armour; on the one hand they had to save the country from the dangers of agitation; on the other, they would not stir until the agitation began. Round this point the controversy between Gladstone and Palmerston began. Morley quotes only part of Palmerston's expression of disapproval on May 12th, but Mr Guedalla has rescued a valuable sentence or two. The speech, said Palmerston, referring to Gladstone's support of Baines on the 11th, "may win Lancashire for you...but I fear it will tend to lose England for you".[1] And he concluded, "It is to be regretted that you should, as you stated, have taken the opportunity of your receiving a deputation of working men, to exhort them to set on foot an agitation for parliamentary reform. The function of a Government is to calm rather than to excite agitation".[2] Apart from the fact that Gladstone had exhorted no one to agitate, the letter creates a feeling in the mind that this attitude towards reform was an absolute impasse. "The function of a government is to calm", says Palmerston; "We will move when the people agitate", said Mr Marsh on the previous day. Gladstone repudiated the charge; after reading the speech and placing it in its true context, we can only say that there was not a shred of evidence to justify Palmerston's accusation. At the conclusion of his speech Gladstone said: "I for myself confess that I think the investigation will be far better conducted if we approach the question at an early date in a calm frame of mind, and without having our doors besieged by crowds or a table loaded with petitions rather than if we postpone entering upon it until a great agitation has arisen".[3] It was a far more statesmanlike view of the function of a government; to calm by action than to attempt to calm by doing nothing, when inaction would be fatal. What exasperated Palmerston most was the breadth of Gladstone's central proposition. It was a pity, Whiteside said, speaking immediately after Gladstone, that Palmerston

[1] Morley, *Life of Gladstone*, vol. I, p. 762.
[2] Conclusion of the letter printed in part by Morley: Guedalla, *Gladstone and Palmerston*, p. 281.
[3] Hansard, vol. CLXXV, 3rd series, May 11th, 1864.

had not been present to deal with the refractory chancellor. Palmerston's absence was to be regretted, we feel, not for that reason alone. He refused to believe that the working classes were at all interested; Baines's and Gladstone's speeches might have corrected that incorrigible attitude. He could write to Gladstone on October 19th, "I think that anybody who looks carefully at the signs of the times must see that there are at present two strong feelings in the national mind, the one a disinclination to organic changes in our representative system".[1] The evidence collected from the industrial areas he ignored to the end; indeed (although he was not opposed to any change) his attitude in 1864 was a vicious circle; a government was a sedative; we need not move only because we refuse to study the signs of the times. The two major charges he brought against Gladstone were, that he would not let sleeping dogs lie, and that his declaration broke faith with the Cabinet. Gladstone denied, in a letter of May 14th, that he had said or done anything to cause an agitation. He had simply said to a deputation, "If you complain of the conduct of Parliament, depend upon it the conduct of Parliament has been connected in no small degree with the apparent inaction or alleged indifference of the working class themselves with respect to suffrage". This was the passage marked by Palmerston, and to this Gladstone replied; there is no doubt when the words are read side by side with the conclusion "Agitation by the working classes on any subject is a thing to be deprecated" and the passage quoted above ("without having our doors besieged

[1] Guedalla, *Gladstone and Palmerston*, p. 297.

by crowds ") that Palmerston's accusation is ground-less.

GLADSTONE to PALMERSTON

11, Carlton House Terrace.

May 14th, 1864.

" I do not see in the passage marked anything in the nature of an exhortation, or anything which goes beyond the nature of a simple recital of what I take to be beyond doubt viz: that among the reasons for the recent inaction of Parliament respecting the franchise has been the allegation, and the belief, that the working classes themselves were indifferent about it.

Mr Cave who preceded me in debate had taken up the strain, and contended that 'nobody desired it'."[1]

PALMERSTON to GLADSTONE

94, Piccadilly.

May 14th, 1864.

" The Deputation said, according to your speech, that they were dissatisfied with Parliament with regard to its conduct about the extension of the Suffrage, and you said to them in reply that the conduct of Parliament in that respect has been connected with the apparent inaction, and alleged indifference of the Working Classes with respect to the Suffrage. It is quite true that you did not use words directly exhorting them to agitate but what you said seems to me to have no other meaning. The case is shortly this, the Deputation say they want an extension of the Suffrage, and are dissatisfied with Parliament for not taking steps to give it them, you say in answer the reason Parliament has done nothing about it is that you have been inactive and are therefore believed to be indifferent. The conclusion obviously is that if they, the

<hr>

[1] Guedalla, Gladstone and Palmerston, p. 284.

working classes, are not indifferent about the Suffrage they ought to cast off that inactivity which has led to their being thought to be indifferent.

I have no doubt that you have yourself heard a great deal about the bad effect of your speech but I can assure you that I hear from many quarters the unfortunate impression it has produced even upon many of the Liberal Party and upon all persons who value the maintenance of our institutions."[1]

The false premise is of course the reference to "inactivity". The next interchange of letters occurred over Gladstone's proposal to publish the speech. He only expresses in words the impression gained by reading the whole debate; that the speech "was talked into importance". It was not in any sense a studied pronouncement, with the intention of compromising the party, but a restrained speech with very definite qualification and explanation of its famous or notorious part.

PALMERSTON *to* GLADSTONE

94, *Piccadilly*,
May 21st, 1864.

" I am told that you are thinking of publishing as a pamphlet with a Preface or Introduction your Speech upon Baines's Motion and I wish to submit for your consideration whether such a course may not be attended with inconvenience as recording in a more formal and deliberate manner that which you said on that occasion.[2] The Government may at some future time have to consider the question of changes in our representation arrangements, though I for one feel well satisfied with things as they are; but if every Member of the Government were now and before hand to pledge himself by

---

[1] Guedalla, *Gladstone and Palmerston*, p. 284.
[2] See note at the end of this section.

premature publication to his own particular views upon a subject with regard to which it is well known that differences of opinion exist, anything like agreement which could only be arrived at by mutual modifications would be rendered impossible, and the day when the subject may be taken up by the Government would be the day fixed for the breaking up of the Administration."[1]

GLADSTONE *to* PALMERSTON

11, *Carlton House Terrace*,
May 23rd, 1864.

"My meaning was this. The speech cannot, I admit, be taken for less than a declaration that, when a favourable state of opinion and circumstances shall arise, the working class ought to be enfranchised to some such extent as was contemplated in the Bill of 1860. But it has been, and is, taken to mean much more.

This accretion, it seems to me, material to get rid of: first for the sake of truth, secondly, to narrow, not to widen any apparent difference between others and myself.

My speech has been talked into importance: and will be quoted: it is desirable I think that this should not be from a text loosely and roughly framed.

In any words I may prefix, I shall derive benefit from what you have written, and will bear it in mind."[2]

The final charge is best answered from Palmerston himself. He wrote on June 16th, 1864, "My view of the general matter is that a member of the Government when he takes office necessarily divests himself of that perfect freedom of individual action which belongs to a private and independent M.P. and the reason is this, that what a member of the government does and says upon public

[1] Guedalla, *Gladstone and Palmerston*, p. 285.
[2] *Ibid.* p. 287.

matters must to a certain degree commit his colleagues ".[1] But he forgot his own position in 1860; what was heinous in a lieutenant was venial or patriotic in the chief. ("It is quite true that the Cabinet, against my advice, came to the decision to go on with your paper duty of customs bill, but I conceive that this does not preclude me or any other member of the Cabinet from representing difficulties and dangers...threatening that course."[2]) (To Gladstone, July 24th, 1860.)

What had Gladstone said? He had first of all, in supporting Mr Baines and replying to Mr Cave, maintained that "the public mind is itself guided and opinion modified in no small degree by the debates of Parliament". To talk of waiting for a popular movement was not only dangerous, it revealed an ignorance of English methods. He proceeded to an estimate of the working class—a favourite theme in these years. What changes they had seen since 1815! "the epoch removed from us in mere chronological reckoning by less than half a century is in the political sphere separated from us by a distance almost immeasurable". One "mathematical demonstration of the competency" of the working classes to discharge important duties, was the co-operative system of Lancashire. It was but further proof "that this generation witnesses the process which unites together not the interests only but the feelings of all the several classes of the community and which throws back into the shadow of oblivion those discords by which they are kept apart from one another". He uttered very wise

[1] Guedalla, *Gladstone and Palmerston*, p. 288.
[2] *Ibid*. p. 147.

words when he contrasted the effects of discontent in different stages of society—distinctions often forgotten by politicians. "An agitation by the working classes is not like an agitation by the classes above them, the classes possessed of leisure. The agitation of those having leisure is easily conducted. It is not with them that every hour of time has a money value." But when the working man was forced to abandon daily labour to agitate "then it is that in railway language the danger signal is turned on" (a quaint phrase in our ears to-day, like the earlier "getting up the steam").

At no time in his career, we believe, unless it was his attitude to Fenianism after 1867, did Gladstone approach a great question with so much wisdom, insight and courage. He possessed the faculty of diagnosis. That he should have been accused, by those who three years before had given way to unreasoning panic, of inciting the working classes was only one among the legion of gross misconceptions endured by him throughout his long life. "Wolf" had been called so often since 1859, that a genuine cry passed unheeded. Of its sincerity and truth there can now be no question. Before the cynics and the fearful, he threw down the gage. The "onus probandi" lay with those who wished to go on excluding forty-nine fiftieths of the working class. And within three years they were brought to the ordeal.

NOTE TO SECTION III

We have seen that Lord Palmerston objected to Gladstone's proposal to publish his speech on Baines's Borough Franchise Bill as a pamphlet with a preface or advertisement. Henry Brand held the same view in a letter written to Gladstone on May 21st, 1864, to which there was an immediate and powerful reply. Both letters are from the Gladstone Papers.

H. BRAND *to* GLADSTONE

" It seems to me that by adopting the form of an advertise- 37 ment you give too much importance to the matter in hand. My notion is that it would be sufficient to apply a short and simple footnote to that sentence in your speech where you say that 'Every man is entitled to the franchise, etc. etc.' The fact is that upon that sentence or rather portion of a sentence the whole fabric of exaggeration has been built up, the press and the public shutting their eyes to the qualifications in the very sentence as well as to the general tenor of your speech. At the same time I am bound to say that the announcement of such a principle startled me. I cannot subscribe to such a principle having always regarded the franchise as a trust and not as a right."

GLADSTONE *to* H. BRAND

May 21st, 1864.

" Very many thanks for your letter. I think what you have 38 said in it shows that there is sufficient cause for something prefatory. For you quote me as saying 'Every man is entitled etc.' But my language as reported is 'morally entitled'. Now it seems to me that the addition of this qualifying word is all-important and that there is no use in passing by the fact that it has been overlooked. I mean all important in reference to the question of abstract right which with you I disclaim. ...I have another purpose in the 'Advertisement'. People say, why all this gratuitous disturbance? I want them to reflect a little, whether it has really been gratuitous or whether there is not a cause."

(iv) *Gladstone and Reform: the Declaration of* 1864

If we were to ask what was most remembered of Gladstone between 1860 and 1866, we should be told that it was the two occasions on which he spoke unwarily; at Newcastle-on-Tyne in 1862, and in the House of Commons in 1864. The Newcastle speech, he acknowledged himself in the later years of his life, to have been a serious error. But his famous declaration of 1864: "I venture to say that every man who is not presumably incapacitated by some consideration of personal unfitness or of political danger, is morally entitled to come within the pale of the constitution" was not a mere indiscretion. It was the result, though he did not admit it at the time, of a long process of development; much of which he revealed during 1866. He had convinced himself by a personal study of working-class districts, and in particular by observing the conduct of one of them, that they were ready to proceed to a higher political level. He became a kind of referee or assessor; and he saw no reason why their supplication should not be answered.

There is no doubt that his sympathy with oppressed peoples abroad came first in order of time, and modified his domestic views. "Parliamentary reform when accompanied by a sympathetic attitude toward Sardinia

(...or towards Greece or Italy...) seemed far more tolerable to him than it had appeared to be shortly before."[1] He began to observe conditions at home with more sympathy. One of his first visits to a great industrial area, an uncommon performance for statesmen then, though Disraeli had shown the way many years before, was to Tyneside. There he made the notorious speech about Jefferson Davis. Another interesting visit, in which Gladstone felt thoroughly at home, was to the Potteries in 1863. This singular district provided him with a congenial theme—the true place of beauty in modern life. There was no occupation which could touch his deepest chords more than that of the designer in Wedgwood's "pot-bank". Greek figures on vases, made in a Pottery suburb called Etruria (a railway station name which still surprises the visitor to those parts) was a fitting subject for this Chancellor of the Exchequer. But it was the merest accident, compared with the true purpose of his visit—to give his support to the working-class interest in culture, and to be identified with the opening of one of the many new popular "Institutes". It was in districts like the Potteries that Gladstone had a new experience. This district in particular, has contrived to cultivate a noble art, though its features are ugly and depressing. Even Bernard Shaw, who hates its face, has not been able to resist its spirit. But what concerns us most was the implication of the visit. Granville and Lowe accompanied him to the "Five Towns", which were once described in an (unpublished) letter as a district far too savage for a youthful candidate. The local

[1] Stanmore, *Life of Sidney Herbert*, vol. II, p. 180.

newspaper, the *Staffordshire Sentinel* was forced to say on December 5th, 1863, "That a Chancellor of the Exchequer should be able to steal time from public duties to descant on the virtues and the labours of a man who was but the humble worker in clay, surely would have been deemed thirty years ago as a startling anomaly". Morley placed the time at an even shorter interval. "In 1863, he was busy in the erection of the post office savings banks. A deputation of a powerful trades-union asked him to modify his rules so as to enable them to place their funds in the hands of the government. A generation before such confidence would have been inconceivable."[1] Gladstone told the Burslem gathering that "they served a nation from whom they might be perfectly assured that their well meant efforts would receive the most cordial and liberal appreciation".[2] And in the same issue, Mr Grenfell, who fought with him side by side in South Lancashire some years later, was reported to have said: "It was impossible for any man, who worked as hard as Gladstone did, not to have sympathy with the working classes throughout the country." By 1864 Gladstone, then, was not indulging in a mere academic theory when he spoke appreciatively of the merits of the working classes. Another event had strengthened the belief which he accepted at first hand, and that was the behaviour of South Lancashire during the American Civil War.

"What are the qualities", Mr Gladstone asked in 1864, "that fit a man for the exercise of a privilege such as the

[1] Morley, *Life of Gladstone*, vol. 1, p. 759.
[2] *Staffordshire Sentinel*, October 31st, 1863.

franchise? Self-command, self-control, respect for order, patience under suffering, confidence in the law, regard for superiors; and when, I should like to ask, were all these great qualities exhibited in a manner more signal, even more illustrious, than in the conduct of the general body of the operatives of Lancashire under the profound affliction of the winter of 1862?"[1]

This was a telling argument. But an even clearer proof of the effect of this "illustrious conduct" on Gladstone, is afforded in a speech—not very well known, which he delivered four years later at Crosby, a small residential district on Liverpool bay, near Seaforth, where his early years were spent.

"In 1865, we asked ourselves what was our duty with reference to reform. We thought that the spirit of order and of loyalty which had developed itself in every part of this country for twenty years and more,—since the Reform Bill of 1832 proved the moral right and title of the labouring population of the country to be admitted to a liberal share. And gentlemen, I must tell you this, because this should come home to your feelings as Lancashire men. If one thing more than another weighed upon my mind in coming to that conclusion, it was the noble, the heroic conduct of the Lancashire operatives during the cotton famine. We felt it was a shame and a scandal that bodies of men such as these should be excluded from the parliamentary franchise."[2]

These words are unmistakeable; and this conviction explains much of what Gladstone said in 1866. What was the effect of this estimate of the stamina of South Lancashire? It was to "elevate his vision" (quoted from

[1] Morley, *Life of Gladstone*, vol. I, p. 758.
[2] At Crosby. Reported in the *Liverpool Post*, November 14th, 1868.

Peel: April 27th, 1866). The position was not the circumscribed or qualified one, which his correspondence with Palmerston in 1864 on this very subject seems to imply. He had reached it by studying facts and making notes; and he could make short work of Lowe's assertion that the house knew nothing about the working class. "Conviction" Gladstone said at Ormskirk on December 19th, 1867; "conviction gentlemen, has placed me in spite of early associations and long cherished prepossessions,—strong conviction and an overpowering sense of the public interest operating for many, many years before full effect was given to it, has placed me in the ranks of the Liberal party".

The clearest statement of all he delivered in the House of Commons on April 27th, 1866; it included another tribute to South Lancashire.

"And now, Sir, let us for a moment consider the enormous and silent changes which have been going forward among the labouring population. May I use the words to honourable and right honourable gentlemen once used by way of exhortation by Sir Robert Peel to his opponents, 'Elevate your vision'? Let us try and raise our views above the fears, the suspicions, the jealousies, the reproaches and the recriminations of this place and this occasion. Let us look onward to the time of our children and of our children's children. Let us know what preparation it behoves us should be made for that coming time. Is there or is there not, I ask, a steady movement of the labouring classes, and is or is not that movement a movement onwards and upwards? I do not say that it falls beneath the eye, for, like all great processes, it is unobservable in detail, but as solid and undeniable as it is resistless in its essential character. It is like those movements of the crust of the earth which science tells us are even now going on in certain portions of the globe. The sailor courses over them in his vessel, and the traveller by land treads them without being conscious of these changes; but from day to day, from hour to hour, the heaving forces are at work, and after a season we discern from actual experience that things are not as they were. Has my right honourable friend, in whom mistrust rises to its utmost height, ever really considered the astonishing phenomena connected with some portion of the conduct of the labouring classes, especially in the Lancashire distress? Has he considered what an amount of self-denial was exhibited by these men in respect to the American war? They knew that the source of their distress lay in the war, yet they never uttered nor entertained the wish that any effort should be made to put an end to it, as they held it to be a war of justice and for freedom. Could any man have believed that a conviction so still, so calm, so firm, so energetic, could have planted itself in the minds of a population without becoming a known patent fact throughout the whole country? But we knew nothing of it. And yet when the day of trial came we saw that noble sympathy on their part with the people of the North; that determination that, be their sufferings what they might, no word should proceed from them that would hurt a cause which they so firmly believed to be just. On one side there was a magnificent spectacle; on the other side was there not also a great lesson to us all, to teach us that in those little tutored, but yet reflective minds, by a process of quiet instillation, opinions and sentiments gradually form themselves of which we for a long time remain unaware, but which, when at last they make their appearance, are found to be deep-rooted, mature and ineradicable?''

"Little tutored "—a phrase coming naturally from him; "yet reflective minds "—the first major acknowledgment in Parliament of the Progress of the working classes during the 'sixties.

In 1865 one step remained to be taken, and Oxford University hastened its accomplishment. The defeat there released him and he moved at once to that part of England where he was always eagerly received, and which had many associations for him. The title page of the edition of *Speeches and addresses delivered at the General Election of* 1865, *by W. E. Gladstone* bears the quotation "He'll shape his old course in a country new". But it was in no spirit of ignorance or uncertainty that he went "unmuzzled" into South Lancashire. He had been convinced by the character of the people that they deserved political rights; no more groundless charge was ever brought against him that his belief in the working classes was a romance. So calm and judicious an observer as Roundell Palmer could write in his *Memorials*,[1]

"No dangerous sentimentality had as yet become a factor in our politics, and there was nothing with which I could not sympathise in Gladstone's phrase, that the men who were to be admitted to a share of power by the enlargement of the franchise were our own flesh and blood. I did not understand it to mean, that they were, for that reason, to have the franchise, but that, being within the limit (whatever it might be) to which the franchise was extended, the common ties of humanity, moral and material, which bound together the several ranks and degrees of the social system and united its members by imperceptible links of mutual interdependence and goodwill, might be relied upon to operate generally, in the long run, in the larger as they had done in the smaller electorate."

This is lawyers' language, but it expressed what Glad-

[1] Lord Selborne, *Memorials*, 2nd series, vol. i, p. 67.

stone meant. "The common ties of humanity" could not be denied; "mutual interdependence" could not be argued away. As Gladstone said, in deciding to reduce the borough franchise, they were doing so, not because of any theory, but because the new electors would justify the "return to an old English principle". And we must remember that it is not those men in history, who having studied the mentality, the intelligence and the qualities of the working class, become disciples of Tom Paine or wish to "Americanise" institutions. These are the sympathies of theorists. Lowe writing to Canon Melville on May 27th, 1865, put his position in a nutshell.

"The first principle is to start unprejudiced and abandon yourself wholly to the teaching of experience. The end being good government, in which of course I include stable government, before I give my assent to the admission of fresh classes, I must be satisfied (not on 'a priori' but on experimental grounds) that their admission will make the government better or more stable."

It is very difficult, almost impossible to carry out experiments in Government. The statesman cannot, like the chemist, when faced with failure, construct a new apparatus and order fresh materials; political mishaps or explosions are difficult to counter. But if there was any sense in which "experimental grounds" could be argued for a reduction of the franchise, it was the data accumulated by an observant and conscientious statesman over many years. Gladstone was "satisfied", both by his visits to industrial areas, and by his readings from the "South Lancashire test" (which was a specimen or type of other areas), that the "experimental" support of the 1866 measure had been demonstrated. Given those qualities in the working man which he enumerated, he believed that his admission would "make the government better and more stable".

This was Gladstone's belief in the working man; what the working man thought of Gladstone after his famous reform speech of 1864 is shown in an address presented to him from the workmen of York. All those stages of development which we have traced were recalled by them, "his services to free trade when he stood by the side of Peel; his budget of 1860; his conspicuous and honourable share in abolishing the taxes on knowledge".

"We have marked your manifestations of sympathy with the down-trodden and oppressed of every clime. You have advanced the cause of freedom in foreign lands by the power and courage with which you have assailed and exposed the misdeeds and cruelties of continental tyrants. To the provident operative you have by your Post Office Savings Bank Bill given security for his small savings, and your Government Annuities Bill of this session is a measure which will stimulate the people to greater thrift and forethought. These acts, together with your speeches on the last named, and on the Borough Franchise Bill, make up a life that commands our lasting gratitude."

No finer proof could be advanced that the statesman who was such an enigma to his peers, had gained the confidence, the understanding and the support of the working classes. He saw their qualities; they applauded his labours. The most powerful force which helped to build up the modern Liberal party was this mutual esteem between Gladstone and the operatives of Great Britain.

CHAPTER VII

THE DEATH OF PALMERSTON
AND ITS EFFECTS

> "It has been assumed by gentlemen that they honour the memory of Lord Palmerston by describing him either generally as the enemy of Reforms, or specially as the enemy of Parliamentary Reform."
>
> Gladstone, April 27th, 1866.

THERE has been a pronounced tendency among writers on the period to describe the death of Palmerston as a catastrophe; the removal of the last moderating influence before the full tide of borough suffrage burst through. In the language of contemporaries too, at the moment of his death, his colleagues "cried 'Havoc' and let slip the dogs of war". The rise of Gladstone no less than that of the elder Pitt was the occasion for misgiving. "Now we shall have no more peace." The number of men who spoke in this strain, and the number of men who have echoed it in writing, is considerable. By taking a few examples from various sources, we shall see the singular unanimity of lamentation; the protecting wall was down.

First, contemporary members of Parliament, Sir Charles Wood is reported to have said as he came from Palmerston's funeral "Our quiet days are over. No more peace for us". In the House of Commons, two distinguished members spoke to the same effect, though their words were much more serious. For they brought a definite charge against Palmerston's senior colleagues —the charge of altering the direction of the Whig party, and of causing a revolution. Speaking in the House of Commons on the Representation of the People Bill, Disraeli said on April 27th, 1866.

"They [i.e. Gladstone] have also a party in the country, not a contemptible party, though I think not a predominant party, and from that moment this party has been at work,— working on the declaration of the Chancellor of the Exchequer [i.e. on Baines's Bill in 1864]. Checked for a moment by the prudence of Lord Palmerston, but the moment he left us, instantly a new character was given to the administration."[1]

The day before, Robert Lowe had referred gravely to the ruin which had overtaken politics since Palmerston was removed. The funeral rites were scarcely over, when his followers struck his flag and discarded his policy.

"Sir, it appears to me", he said, "we have more and more reason every day we live to regret the loss of Lord Palmerston. The remaining members of his government would seem, by way of a mortuary contribution to have buried in his grave all their prudence, statesmanship and moderation. He was scarcely withdrawn from the scene before they set to work to contravene and contradict his policy. I suppose they must have thought that the best way to secure a continuance of that success was to aim at doing that which he above all other things disapproved. The noble lord at the head of the Government and the right honourable gentleman the Chancellor of the Exchequer have performed a great feat. They have taken the great mass of their supporters and laid them at the feet of the honourable member for Birmingham."

Both the general and the concluding particular charge

[1] Hansard, 3rd series, vol. 183, p. 80.

were tremendous. Bright's influence, as we shall show, was undoubtedly strong in 1866, and Lowe, though striking out blindly, came near to the truth. At the moment we are concerned with the sweeping indictment; that Russell and Gladstone had thrown off the bonds, imposed, we are to understand, by Palmerston. The mourning of 1865 and 1866 passed through natural stages until it became a sentimental romance. Frequently in English history has the trump of doom sounded; but "Ichabod" was never so plain at the passing of one man. "Lord Palmerston had died and with him old England."[1] "During Lord Palmerston's life, the question of Reform to which that popular statesman was personally hostile had been allowed to slumber."[2] To the Queen indeed, the passing of Palmerston, though a "double bereavement", did not mean the end of all things. "This is another link with the past which is broken...the Queen feels deeply" (October 19th, 1865). "The happy past—which is gone" (October 20th) had no political meaning; husband and first minister gone—that was the Queen's feeling. She was far from sharing the fears of others, that the death of Palmerston would introduce a restless era of change.[3] The Prince Consort had left her interested in reform, and she accepted Russell's proposals as a normal and necessary stage, with the warning "it must be very carefully framed (the Ministry's Reform Bill),

[1] Lang, *Stafford Northcote*, p. 137.
[2] *Life of Gathorne-Hardy*, p. 183.
[3] Cf. "Disraeli's comment on the Queen's Speech was that it convicted the world of great injustice to Lord Palmerston, who it would now seem, was probably the most ardent reformer in his Cabinet" (February 5th, 1866). Lang, *Stafford Northcote*, p. 141.

so that it should not again fail, as it had done on two previous occasions " (October 29th, 1865). Nevertheless, the death of Palmerston and the policy of Lord Russell's ministry introduced a new theme. Stated bluntly the charge is this: Russell and Gladstone were waiting their chance; they dared not introduce a Reform Bill during Palmerston's lifetime. The moment he was dead, they did their worst.

Now this charge is part of a great indictment, treated elsewhere, that the desire for reform was artificially created. It is largely answered by considering the attitude of the working classes towards reform throughout the 'sixties, and while Palmerston was still alive and in power. What we have to consider now is only a part of the true bill; it is a personal matter, a concern of individuals (where the indictment as a whole is a question of forces), and it is best met and answered at the moment of Palmerston's death. We know that Palmerston strongly criticised Gladstone's attitude in 1864; what we have to examine is the suggestion that the Chancellor of the Exchequer's loyalty, up to 1865, was insincere and simulated.

The most convincing answer lies in part of one of Gladstone's greatest speeches. Replying at the end of the debate on the second reading of the Reform Bill of 1866 (April 27th), he dealt with the accusation that the subject before the House was in itself a treachery to his late leader; and he dealt with it immediately on rising. Among the many charges brought against the Liberals during the long debate, none had stung him more than this.

"In the first place, I must presume to say a word upon the subject of the references which have been made to a great name among us in this House and in the country—I mean the name of Lord Palmerston. It has been assumed by gentlemen...that they honour the memory of Lord Palmerston by describing him either generally as the enemy of Reforms, or specially as the enemy of Parliamentary Reform. Or again, and yet more specifically, by describing him especially as the enemy of that which constitutes the essential point and the very hinge of the whole framework of this Bill—namely, a reduction of the borough franchise. Now, Sir, to throw light upon this subject, I will read but a few words which Lord Palmerston used in supporting his own Bill in 1860. He said, that the provisions of that Bill were open, as without doubt the provisions of our Bill and of every other Bill, are open, to consideration in Committee; but he went on to use these words 'there are certain fundamental principles in the bill which we could not consent to have infringed, because that would destroy the measure altogether'. One main principle of the Bill is, the reduction of the borough franchise. It has been assumed by some speakers, that the life of Lord Palmerston was a security against the introduction of a measure of reform. I think it no less due to Lord Palmerston than to his colleagues to say that, as far as I am aware—and I presume the right honourable gentleman will admit that if mischief of any kind had been brewing in the Cabinet, I probably should have known it—there never was a difference of opinion between Lord Palmerston and his colleagues on the question of Reform."

Gladstone went on to discuss the reasons why reform had been shelved since 1860—"I know of no member of the Cabinet of Lord Palmerston who ever thought that, after the abandonment of that measure, and considering the circumstances which prevailed from the

115   8-2

year 1860, down to the dissolution of last year, it would have been wise or warrantable for the Cabinet to have revived the subject of Reform ". (There were sufficient reasons in the state of foreign affairs. Indeed, foreign affairs provided an impetus on two occasions to the working class interest in reform associations—the Polish Rising and the visit of Garibaldi.) Coming to the 1865 election, the speaker went on—they

"had brought again before us the very occasion on which it was our duty to become responsible for another measure of reform. Nor have we the smallest right, the smallest ground, to suppose that Lord Palmerston differed from that opinion. We cannot, indeed, say that he agreed in it; and why? Because, at the moment of his lamented death, no single Cabinet had been held for the purpose of considering the measure to be adopted during the coming Session. But I do chance to know, and it is a posthumous record of some interest, that Lord Palmerston had a conversation with one, at least, of his colleagues at no very long period before his death—it may have been a twelvemonth, or even more; I cannot further define the time—on this very subject. I have not the smallest doubt in my mind, though I cannot state it as a matter of fact, that he was looking forward to the dissolution as the critical period when a fresh decision would have to be taken. In that consideration he stated his opinion that within a limited time it would be right for the government again to introduce the subject of Reform. So much, Sir, for the honour of Lord Palmerston ".

So much, too, for the honour of Gladstone. Though his denial of the charge was not supported by chapter and verse, it must be allowed to carry with it the weight of authority. After all, the defence is far more substantial than the accusation. Gladstone's character and his position as a Cabinet Minister give the answer conviction. Palmerston, on several occasions, pointed out that he found difficulty in measuring the possible consequences of a renewal of interest in the subject in the country. He feared "swamping". But he must have been wise enough, as is obvious from Mr Guedalla's selection of letters, to perceive the amount of interest, the amount of organisation and the amount of machinery possessed by the working classes, to make, at any moment, a pressing question of reform. He was not the man to shirk a responsibility of that kind. It must be repeated that the number and character of reform associations were sufficient to bring the question to the front at any moment. The truth seems to be, not that his death released these forces, but that it took place when they were ready to operate. Bearing in mind Gladstone's speech, the assertion that after Palmerston came the deluge is untenable. On July 8th, 1864, replying to the motion of censure moved by Disraeli, Palmerston criticised the way in which Russell's foreign policy had been discussed. He was as much responsible, he said, as the Foreign Minister. He repudiated the idea that the responsibility was divided. We must also refuse to separate his name from the subject of reform in 1865; and, by so doing, clear the name of Gladstone.

CHAPTER VIII

THE REFORM BILLS OF 1866 AND 1867

"I believe that those persons whom we ask you to enfranchise ought rather to be welcomed as you would welcome recruits to your army or children to your family."

Gladstone, March 12th, 1866.

(i) *The Ministry of Russell. Character of the Conflict*

LORD RUSSELL kissed hands as Prime Minister at 10 o'clock on the morning of October 29th, 1865; the reform of the Parliament was the first matter discussed. The Queen said that the Prince Consort "had always wished that a moderate measure of reform should be proposed and carried when there was no excitement or clamour for it in the country; but that it must be very carefully framed, so that it should not again fail, as it had done on two previous occasions".[1] Despite the pressure of many weighty events—the Jamaica Insurrection, the Cattle Plague, and the financial panic in the city—parliamentary reform occupied almost the whole attention of the ministry until it collapsed in the summer of 1866. The Prime Minister and Gladstone gave the matter all their energy and enthusiasm. "If I bring in or contribute to bring in a measure," wrote Russell to Gladstone on January 25th, 1866, "it will be to me a satisfactory close of my political life—whether carried or defeated*." His lieutenant assured him of his loyalty; a perfect understanding existed between the two men. "We cannot

[1] *Letters of Queen Victoria*, 2nd series, vol. I, p. 281.

118

communicate too often, too fully or too unreservedly. With the excellent spirit that prevails, I feel sure you will get through your work*" (Gladstone to Russell, October 24th, 1865).

In this frame of mind, they began their work. We consider the history of reform in 1866 and 1867 as an example of a brilliant parliamentary contest, of a new type of agitation in the country. In 1866, the relations between Gladstone and Russell are of considerable importance; and when Russell passes from the leadership, the final event of interest is the history of the Liberal party in 1867.

The Character of the Conflict. One of the greatest episodes in the history of the House of Commons was now about to open; an episode which has undeservedly passed into oblivion, and which even the lovers of good English prose have made little attempt to rescue. The great Reform Battle of 1866–7 is a profound reminder of the ephemeral and transient fame of the most brilliant passages at arms in Parliament. Statesmen speak on the burning question of the hour; the hour passes and their words are forgotten. Asquith truly described Hansard as "a graveyard"; a few epitaphs live in the shape of classic phrases which are incorporated into the language. We remember that session now, more for what it added to our vocabulary, than for what it added to our constitution. It is a singular and remarkable thing too, that in the fight where so many ideas and principles were borrowed and appropriated, there should have been so much verbal plagiarism. The word with which Gladstone thrilled the Free Trade Hall at Manchester was not his but Palmerston's.[1] Bright employed the figure of Adullam, used before him by his great American friend; and Derby's "Leap in the Dark" was a borrowed phrase. But the chief interest in the years 1866–7, nevertheless, remains their oratory. The whole encounter presented a glittering array of talent; a fertility of resource and tactics, alarms and excursions, which have always appeared in the greatest dramas of the Commons. It is a type; a classic example of the qualities of politicians and parties; of the irresponsibility of the genius and the disciplined small men, of the champion trying a throw with his antagonist. Every feature we expect in the greatest meetings of the English Parliament is here. In eloquence, in invective, in manœuvre, it ranks with the Corn Law Debates, the battle over Bradlaugh and the stormy career of the Home Rule Bills. The ingenuity of the skirmish, the fertility of amendment and resolution, the appeal to broad principle and the sifting of minutiae, all help to make this session a dominating obelisk in the oratorical "graveyard". And apart from the qualities which we instinctively expect, above and beyond the normal flora and fauna of debate, flourish the more rarified creations of speech and scruple, which have, at long periods, made the passing of a bill through Parliament a magnificent affair. There are great desertions; there is much lamentation over the glory that is departing. Some of the speeches are worthy to rank among the greatest efforts in the English tongue, reaching high-water mark. Gladstone and Lowe were the outstanding pair. No finer peroration has ever been heard in Parlia-

[1] Lord Oxford, *Fifty Years of Parliament*, vol. II, p. 228.

ment than the invocation of those "great social forces which move onwards in their might and majesty". Even on the tombstone these words have a compelling authority; and their effect on the Commons, wearied with long hours of technicalities, was acknowledged even by foes to have been overwhelming. Lowe caught the mutter of the host without also. But the music beat more heavily on his ears. The solemn warning, the prophetic note which Lowe uttered, places him among the array of ghosts who through two centuries have foretold the destruction of Parliament and the doom of England. With Wellington and with Rosebery, Lowe weeps over Jerusalem. Rosebery's words on the Parliament Act: "I wish therefore in the final farewell, that my voice at least, shall be raised for the last time in a definite protest against this most ill-judged, revolutionary and partisan measure"; recall in a striking manner Lowe's peroration:

"Surely the heroic work of so many centuries; the matchless achievements of so many wise heads and strong hands, deserve a nobler consummation than to be sacrificed at the shrine of revolutionary passion, or the maudlin enthusiasm of humanity. But if we do fall, we shall fall deservedly.... History may tell of other acts as signally disastrous, but of none more wanton, none more disgraceful".

No more convincing tribute to the strength of the English Constitution could be offered than these two solemn knells separated by half a century. Lowe, who had at one time been the Hampden of Sydney, was possessed with a genuine fear of the democracy. A man who could not understand a classical allusion was little better than a bushman. He refused to accept the *onus probandi*. Suppose men have the rights you claim, he said in substance; the English Parliament still exists to decide the time and extent of the instalments of liberty. In a scornful reference to the Greek cities of antiquity "whose domestic squabbles occupied the youth of honourable members", the most brilliant classic in the Commons denied the ability, and with it the right, of the masses to order their own affairs. But Lowe was not intellectually as well as physically short-sighted; he was one of the first to realise that his masters would need education. Disraeli, Bright and Mill also reached a high level; though Mill, the only purely logical and philosophical reasoner throughout the debates, rarely exercised the authority in the Commons which is enjoyed by those who have served their apprenticeship there. Not in oratory alone, not in the wealth of theory and political philosophy alone, were the reform debates a type of the English Parliament in full working order. No parliamentary drama has been complete without a great desertion. Disraeli mocking Peel; the "treachery" of Joseph Chamberlain—these are the stirring episodes. No less momentous was the "cave of Adullam". Lowe was doing for Russell and Gladstone what Disraeli had done for Peel. He did not, however, ruin the ministers of the party, but he very nearly ruined himself. With the exception of Ayrton, he was the most unpopular member of the first Gladstone ministry. The fame of his speeches passed as quickly as it had arisen (he was given a magnificent reception at Oxford in 1866); and it was fortunate for him that he did not suffer the fate of Randolph

Churchill (Gladstone contrived to save him "from the ruck of official barons "). There were desertions in 1867, but those of 1866 were more picturesque and dramatic.

The struggle in the country after the session of 1866 was of a new type; though the 1868 election completed the evolution, the country had shown, two years earlier, how true an estimate Gladstone had formed of the working classes. In the early nineteenth century a public meeting is first an act of sedition, an occasion for the appearance of the military. In the 'forties, an attempt is made to give a tone of respectful supplication to all popular agitation. The Chartists march to Westminster with their petition; and even then, as at Newport, the old method of breaking heads dies hard. The platforms of Cobden and Bright are modern in design. Thousands assemble to listen to statistics and to frame resolutions and petitions. The working class gained much political self-consciousness from the Anti-Corn Law campaign. But Bright and Cobden were not ministers, were not in the front rank. The agitation of 1866 and 1867 is the first expression by the country as a whole, of its opinions and its demands, in the modern manner. The petitioners do not come up; the minister goes down to the petitioners. The audience is respectable, sure of itself, and sure of its champions. There is not a single resolution which does not express confidence in Gladstone, Bright and Mill. This is a curious trinity, but the people know their men. When the Park railings came down, the conduct of the crowd was eminently Victorian. There was material enough for a dozen Peterloos; but those days were gone. There was very little, practically none, of the indiscriminate violence and unsolicited assistance of professional hooligans which would have characterised a London gathering forty years before. The effect of the Hyde Park incident was considerable enough to make Disraeli plead that reform was not a party measure. And it cannot be denied that Holyoake and Beales were professionally engaged agitators, the one of the Cobbett, the other of the Place or Girdlestone type. Satirical newspapers like *The Tomahawk* denounced Beales with a vehemence which does not disguise their fear of his influence. But on the whole the agitation was thoroughly modern. The meetings are the same in character, intention and conduct, as those which met to denounce Bulgarian and Armenian atrocities. A new type of member was appearing also. In his *Thirty Years of Parliament*, McCullagh Torrens, the distinguished member for Finsbury who did so much for the unification of London, reveals the working of a constituency in a thoroughly modern way. Sitting for the first time in the Parliament which met after the death of Palmerston, he studied minutely the conditions of his constituency and the opinions of his constituents. Like Forster, he was first of all a capable man at the desk; but he shared with Forster, whom he resembles in possessing safe capacity of the second rank, the ability to mount the platform, and load a compelling speech with facts and figures.

Such a character had the struggle which opened in 1866; Parliament gave a display of its highest powers; and afterwards the great meeting, composed of working men who knew their need, exerted a pressure upon it.

THE REFORM BILLS OF 1866 AND 1867

(ii) *Gladstone and the Reform Bill of* 1866

The year 1866 was for Gladstone a time of intense activity and incessant strain. Believing that the hour had come when "to carry enfranchisement below the present line was essential to character, credit and usefulness" (Speech, March 12th, Introducing Bill), he made the cause of reform his chief work. Both he and Russell were deeply interested in the measure; Gladstone, because he had formed a new estimate of the working classes; Russell, because there could be no more fitting climax to a lifelong interest in the measure. But, from the start, they were faced with great difficulties; between March and June every conceivable type of opposition and obstruction was applied against them. They were equally exercised as to what course to pursue against their adversaries and what fate to choose for their administration. But the sincerity and honesty of both men throughout this grim struggle are unquestionable. It left an ineffaceable mark upon Gladstone. Though he had nothing whatever to do with the popular agitation in the summer and autumn, the people at last hailed him, with no uncertain voice, as their champion. "He crossed the Rubicon"; and Disraeli never showed a more complete misunderstanding of the character of his antagonist than when he said it was their business to help the right honourable gentleman to retrace his steps and build new boats in place of those he had burnt. The story of this stormy session has been described in many biographies; and we have been told of a score of parties held during that spring which met to dine and remained to discuss, to intrigue and to conspire. Yet this very season, when events moved by the minute, occupies only a few pages of Morley's narrative. It was natural to expect a store of letters at Hawarden which would throw light on the details of the battle. A search revealed a considerable number from Russell—which prove his sincerity beyond doubt; several from Bright, who took up the rôle of critic and remembrancer to the ministry; and one or two others from lesser men of a party interest. It is not our business to steer through this Sargasso Sea of amendments and motions; but to give a general survey of the conduct of the Prime Minister and his lieutenant from the beginning of the year until they finally went down to Windsor on June 26th. What has been said elsewhere refutes a suggestion that "Russell's main object in proposing fresh reforms was not so much the welfare of the people as the rehabilitation of his own party".[1] This is only another example of that type of analysis which insists that certain statesmen were out to make their own fortunes by the desperate expedient of ruining the firm. These new letters of Russell silence the voice of criticism. But they also give us a glimpse of a Gladstone hard pressed, beset on every side. In his life he endured a dozen stern battles that would have broken anyone of smaller stature; and he emerges from this one, the conscientious minister and the loyal colleague, though a sorely tried man.

Russell's note at the beginning of the year was one of optimism. On the first day of the new year he wrote to Gladstone:

[1] E. H. Dance, *The Victorian Illusion*, p. 34.

126

"I think £6 rateable value would do and I will send you 41
a table tomorrow to show the effect. As writing makes a
correct man, I am writing my thoughts on this important
and urgent subject" (it was important and urgent enough to
finish his ministry). "I think we can have a good measure
by which we can stand or fall—I will not venture to say which
it will be."

And to Charles Wood on February 7th in the same strain:
"Altogether the opening prospects seem bright".[1] One
shadow indeed was thrown early over his hopes; but
throughout the month he was not fearful of the future.
Gladstone echoed his optimism.

"Without attempting to calculate the personal uncer- 42
tainties which may attend the future, I can assure you that
my disposition is, in the matter of the franchise; first, to attach
a great weight to your judgment and secondly, to adopt the
£6 rating as being, in so far as our present knowledge goes,
decidedly the best and fairest basis on which we can take our
stand. I confidently hope to fight out this battle by your
side" (Gladstone to Russell, January 25th).

Russell acknowledged the resolve. "I am very much 43
obliged to you for your letter of this morning, notwith-
standing the efforts of Lowe, Elcho and Delane" (a
trinity of unregenerates!). "I have very good hopes of
success*." But it was not from these three men who had
not changed their opinions over ten years that the first
criticism came, but from Bright. He will live for ever
in our political history as the man who hated the policy
of taking questions by halves. Over India, over Ireland,
over the suffrage, he bitterly opposed reform by instalments. Just as it was not enough to reform the Church

[1] Gooch, *Later Correspondence of Lord John Russell*, vol. 2, p. 343.

of Ireland without reforming the tenure of land, it was insufficient to admit new electors without redistribution. Even in "glad confident morning", Russell warned Grey, "I feel grave doubts about the proposal not to touch the seats. Bright has shown his cards and if we follow suit we shall be considered his partners" (this happened, although Russell wished to postpone the question of seats until the next year). "I begin to fear we must have some partial disfranchisement";[1] but he hoped, "with Stansfeld and Forster standing by the government bill, the Bright discontented party will be reduced to small dimensions".[2] A few hours after this was written, Bright opened the attack on Gladstone himself; "a few thousand electors more or less are of no consequence", but let us have the Bill.

> *4, Hanover Street, Hanover Square,*
> *February 10th, 1866.*

44 "Dear Mr Gladstone,

I think I mentioned to you that in Scotland there is now what may be termed a 'lodger franchise'.

Mr M'Laren, the Member for Edinburgh, is acquainted with it thoroughly, and I think you should see him. I know how busy you must be—but this question presses, and I am anxious for you to see him. If convenient for you I would come with him to see you on Monday, or on any other day, at any hour that may be least inconvenient to you, and which you may fix upon.

The delay of the Government in deciding upon their bill and in bringing it into the House will I fear damage you greatly. Bouverie and all who are angry at being left out of

---

[1] Russell to George Grey, January 7th. Gooch, *Later Correspondence of Lord John Russell*, vol. 2, p. 343.

[2] Russell to Charles Wood, February 7th. Gooch, *op. cit.* p. 343.

your office arrangements, will do all the mischief they can, and the whole concern will become disorganised before the Bill is before us.

You have had three months in which to frame a bill, which any man knowing anything of the subject, could have done in a week—and the Bill is not only not drawn, but its very purpose and extent are not yet determined.

You have been hunting for figures from Parish Officers to prove how many working men are now electors—as if a great question like this were to be decided in a huckstering spirit, and as if a few thousand of Electors more or less were of the smallest consequence.

I venture to predict injury to the cause and a wreck of the administration if this miserable indecision is continued. Sir George Grey spoke last night as if terrified of naming the subject of Reform, and the Tories look on with delight, at the evidence of incapacity and irresolution in every action of the Government in regard to it.

This is friendly criticism, if not pleasant. I think you are digging your own political graves—and *I lament it bitterly*. If you wish to see Mr M'Laren, one line from me will be enough.

Always faithfully yours,

J. BRIGHT."

Gladstone sent the letter on to Russell, with a note: "I enclose for your edification a note from Bright, full of sugar plums" (February 10th).

But the ministers were far busier than Bright supposed; Russell seems to have been completely convinced by now that a complementary scheme of redistribution must occupy their minds.

"Here is another point of more consequence", he urged **45** on February 23rd. "My mind after consulting sensible men and feelings on the subject of redistribution is this. I think it enough reason for our present course that a dissolution would not be necessary for two or three years after the passing of our bill, and that if we disfranchise and enfranchise, a dissolution this year would be inevitable. Now sudden dissolutions after a short interval are in themselves evils. But on the other hand, I fear that some disfranchisement and some enfranchisement is absolutely necessary, in order to give permanence to our settlement. The necessity of it is rooted in the reforming and also perhaps in the conservative mind of England—the Liberals go upon this theory of representation, the Tories on the practical gain of a few more seats for counties. That being so I would say in spirit, though not in terms—the Government will consider next year the question of redistribution and propose after that consideration a measure on the subject. But if the House of Commons is of opinion that the measure must be introduced this year with the penalty of immediate dissolution attached to it, we will give our best thoughts to it and introduce such a measure in a fortnight " (to Gladstone).

On this subject, Russell was accommodating, because political small talk had pushed it to the front. It had now become obvious that the struggle would be stern; if redistribution meant dissolution what would the Liberals say? On the other hand, no redistribution gave the
46 enemy a formidable weapon. "We cannot", he wrote again on February 26th, "any more than the old man with the ass please everybody. One set of gentlemen say 'We cannot vote for our own dissolution', another set say 'We cannot vote for you unless you deal with seats', which would clearly make dissolution this year necessary. I think you can put this point clearly in your speech*" (to Gladstone). The speech released all those elements

of opposition which were in readiness. "I believe", said Gladstone introducing the bill on March 12th, "that those persons whom we ask you to enfranchise ought rather to be welcomed as you would welcome recruits to your army or children to your family." One great man utterly denied that any recruits were needed; Lowe was absolutely sincere in his opposition, he had nothing to gain and much to lose. Perhaps he was the only man, beside Gladstone, who had set himself to study the question of a "fitness" qualification, while other men haggled over the margin of a pound or two. That study had driven the two men to extreme opposites of opinion. Both were disinterested. (There was no question of Lowe joining the opposition; and Bright's epithet "The Cave" at least clears from the name any suspicion of intrigue.) As Brand wrote to Russell, March 29th, "Horsman and Lowe can no more coalesce with Disraeli and company than vinegar with oil. If anything can ruin you it will be Bright's patronage".[1] Lowe attacked with the vigour of an honest enemy, and he had a foeman worthy of his steel. But his opposition was the signal for some inglorious operations; sedition spread fast. The standard raised for lofty motives became the rallying place for many men who loved power and security first. There is an entry in Northcote's diary which shows how quickly the disaffection spread.

"*March* 14. Dined with Cardwell. Forster was there and talked freely of the Reform Bill, with which he said he was agreeably disappointed. He had expected to be obliged to leave the Government when it should be announced, but now

[1] Gooch, *Later Correspondence of Lord John Russell*, vol. 2, p. 344.

thought the £7 franchise would be accepted by the Liberals as a compromise. He thought Lowe's and Horsman's violent speeches would reconcile the Liberals to this high figure, by showing them that it was a measure of sufficient importance to cause a panic, and that it might be taken as a settlement for our lifetime."[1]

It was not, as events proved, the measure but those same violent speeches which made the extra-mural demand insistent and beat down the original £7 to household suffrage. But at the moment there was no panic. Gladstone snatched a few days from parliamentary work to go down and speak in South Lancashire; but the issue remained for the time being a House of Commons one. The first of the series of counter-moves had to be faced (Grosvenor's Motion on Redistribution) and Gladstone bore the brunt. He was already feeling the strain.

"I think we want rather more help than we get in considering the details from some of the less worked members of the Cabinet. Statistics, points of law, new suggestions, every sort of thing flows in upon me and it is difficult to bring all straight, with some fourteen hours daily of other work. I am anxious, for the crisis is really great, that nothing should be lost through want of consideration" (to Russell, April 14th).[2]

"Toiling terribly" as he did from the beginning to the end of his life. Russell replied, exhorting him to be of good courage; but we catch, at the same time, the first note of warning. "We may have a question in the further progress of the Bill, in which we may be defeated and the alternatives in that case—submit, resign, dissolve.

47

[1] Lang, *Stafford Northcote*, p. 153.
[2] Gooch, *Later Correspondence of Lord John Russell*, vol. 2, p. 345.

But all will depend on the question involved. Only let us not resolve beforehand to submit or indeed to resign*" (Russell to Gladstone, April 16th).

A singular and memorable episode followed, and we think that in no other country, save England, could it have happened. In the middle of the party fight the great debate on redistribution took place. The Tory attitude was that the original bill was incomplete; but the subject of the debate is obscured by its character. Several statesmen reached a high table-land of oratory. Lowe was supreme. He gave Bright no quarter. "Demagogues", he said, "are the commonplace of history. He invited household suffrage and it has come. You can never stop when once you set the ball rolling. Democracy you may have at any time. Night and day the gate is open that leads to that bare and level plain." He denounced Mill's theory of the inevitability of universal suffrage as "a seemingly harmless dream that puts the dagger into the hand of the assassin". It was "the coward's argument". Gladstone wound up the debate with one of his greatest speeches. He answered the words of the motion: "My belief is that redistribution though an exceedingly important subject, is secondary altogether to the franchise, because it is limited by and regulated upon principles which I think afford little room for difference of opinion among fair-minded and moderate men" (April 27th). He concluded: "The banner which we now carry in this fight, though perhaps at some moment it may droop over our sinking heads yet it soon will float in the eye of heaven and it will be borne by the firm hands of the united people of the three kingdoms, perhaps not to an easy, but to a certain and to a not distant victory ". Despite the magnificent appeal, the banner drooped. Encouragement now came from a more illustrious quarter, qualified by the hope that the ministers would not endanger the honour of the administration by standing firm to their original scheme. No one desired a settlement more than the Queen—but it was not the kind of settlement talked of by the opposition.

"The Queen...must express her anxious hope that Lord Russell will give its due weight to the evident feeling of the House of Commons and that in determining not to abandon the Queen's service, he will be careful to avoid anything which, from an idea that the honour and consistency of the Government would require it, might have the effect of shutting the door to such a settlement of this most difficult question (even if it should not be possible to effect it in the course of this Session) as may be accepted by all Parties "[1] (to Russell, April 29th, 1866).

[It is interesting to note that the same idea had been in

48 Gladstone's mind only a few days previously. "The Amalgamation of the Two Bills (Franchise and Distribution) unless accompanied by an autumn session would be another cause for postponement till next year. I distinctly adverted to the idea of an autumn session— not a man noticed it*" (Gladstone to Russell, April 23rd).] Russell, however, had realised by now that the Tories would not wait. He sent on the Queen's "noble" letter to Gladstone.

49 "I send you a letter of the Queen who has great influence with me—but I think as the Tories would not trust us till next session, it is impossible that we with much stronger

[1] *Letters of Queen Victoria*, 2nd series, vol. I, p. 324.

grounds of distrust, can keep the question in abeyance till next session in the hope that the Tories finding we had quenched all the zeal of our supporters would become suddenly conciliatory and yielding" (Russell to Gladstone, April 30th).

What was the feeling in the country while the fate of the ministry was being discussed? It agreed with the Queen in one particular; it gave contrary counsel in another. "Stand firm", it said, "but if you are defeated, dissolve. Then a greater voice will speak." We have proof of this in a letter and enclosure from Forster written on May 11th.

Colonial Office.
May 11th, 1866.

"Dear Mr Gladstone,   **50**

At the request of the Bradford National Reform Union, I beg to hand you the accompanying Resolutions they have passed in relation to the Redistribution of Seats Bill. I have reason to believe that these Resolutions represent the feeling and views of the Reformers of Bradford.

I am, dear Mr Gladstone,

Yours very faithfully,

W. E. FORSTER."

(The letter is endorsed "Resolutions of the Bradford Union, who are willing to accept the Redistribution Bill as a compromise, although it is not sufficiently comprehensive; but they urge the Government not to give way in any point in either of the Bills and to dissolve if defeated".)

Enclosure:

RESOLUTION OF THE COMMITTEE OF THE NATIONAL REFORM UNION, BRADFORD BRANCH, MAY 9TH, 1866.

"That while the Bill for the redistribution of seats leaves very much to be desired, inasmuch as it does not include within the proposed groups of Boroughs, many towns, hitherto unrepresented, which might well have been included in these groups, and that it also still leaves wholly unrepresented many large towns fairly entitled to send members to Parliament, this Committee nevertheless desires to express its unabated confidence in the Government and to support the ministry in carrying this measure as a compromise, but would respectfully urge upon the Government to adhere firmly to its provisions, and not to suffer, either in the case of this bill, or in that for the extension of the suffrage, any change in the direction of making either of these measures less liberal.

This committee would further press upon the Government that in the event of defeat upon either of these bills, they should not hesitate to appeal to the country by a dissolution of Parliament."

RT. HON. W. E. GLADSTONE, M.P.

Chancellor of H.M. Exchequer.

These are very prosaic assassins! But the Government was fast coming to the conclusion that the tactics of the opposition demanded that they should face the problem. They were now carrying on a guerilla warfare; and the Chancellor of H.M. Exchequer was becoming exhausted, both by "the combined measure" and by the attacks on different fronts. In the next two months the opposition tried to insert anti-bribery clauses, expressed dissatisfaction at the "grouping", and finally wished to damn the Government by the faint praise of general resolutions of confidence. Gladstone, in the thickest of the fight, cried aloud for reinforcements.

51   "I have several times urged the necessity of some arrangement in the Cabinet for looking to all the points that arise

upon the Reform Bill. The matter has now reached a point
at which I think we shall get into utter confusion unless
prompt measures are adopted. The Franchise Bill alone I
might have managed, but to arrange, put into shape and
prepare for the Cabinet, the multitude of points that arise
upon the combined measure is physically as well as in every
other way impossible for me,—nor do I see how it can be
done unless a small committee of the Cabinet will undertake
the responsibility of doing this work" (Gladstone to Russell,
May 28th).

It must have been a Herculean task that made Gladstone
shrink. While he was still busy on the fortifications, the
enemy and the mutineers made the first of that series of
assaults which finally won the stronghold and in which
they were themselves to be besieged. On June 1st Russell
wrote in disgust at Captain Hayter's Resolution. It is
"unworthy of a great party. Mr Pitt said the first quality 52
required in an English minister was patience, and
certainly there is great scope for that quality at the
present time.... Their word (the Tories) is not to be
depended upon as Sir Robert Peel's was at the time of
the First Reform Bill*" (Russell to Gladstone, June 1st).
The end soon came; not even the fact that "the Queen 53
is naturally biassed now by the desire for political ease*"
(Gladstone to Russell, June 11th) was sufficient to alter
the conviction of the ministers. An amendment of
Lord Dunkellin's to substitute rating for rental was
carried against the Government on June 15th by a
majority of eleven. The deciding factor was Gladstone
and he would go no further. It had become obvious that
there was no sincere desire in the Commons for reform,
and whatever turn events took the Government was

bound to be humiliated. The Queen and the Editor of *The Times* wished the Government to remain, but every suggestion was repugnant to Gladstone.

"I hope...you will not think it necessary to act upon a hasty and evidently ill-considered phrase or two of Mr Gladstone's in last night's debate...and break up a ministry... on account of a paltry defeat on an amendment to a clause in Committee proposed by one of your ordinary supporters. I am quite sure that, if you were to withdraw the reform bill, pledging yourselves to bring in another next year, and challenge the opposition to a vote of want of confidence, you would have a large majority"[1] (Delane to Clarendon, June 19th, 4 a.m.).

Clarendon replied that "Disraeli and Stanley are *wild for office*" and that "the loot is, I believe, all distributed". Gladstone saw clearly that the vote of confidence plan would be a retrograde and inglorious one. "I wish I could see my way about a vote of confidence. A general declaration for reduction of the franchise would land us where we were in April, 1859" (Gladstone to Russell, June 22nd).[2] Time was on his side, but he would not put the clock back after so exacting a battle. There can be no doubt that Gladstone's view precipitated, even determined, the resignation. After Dunkellin's Amendment, Russell appears to have been open minded on the question. He was as optimistic in June and July as he was in January. In considering resignation, he would 54 forbear "while speaking strongly from uttering any threats*" (to Gladstone, June 18th). It seems too that he realised, before Gladstone, that the country was at

[1] Dasent, *Life of Delane*, vol. 11, p. 169.
[2] Gooch, *Later Correspondence of Lord John Russell*, vol. 2, p. 351.

last aroused. On June 21st, he wrote again: "If we are 55 to go into opposition, we must keep up our Reform Flag; the failures you mention from 1857 to 1866 have been caused by the hostility of the House of Commons, and the apathy of the people. No government can force reform on an unwilling nation, but the feeling improves every day*" (Russell to Gladstone). It is singular that Russell observed what was happening in the country— we hear the same assurance from him again—while Gladstone remained silent. Was he blind, at the moment, to the movement among the great social forces because he was outraged by their representatives? At all events, he bid strongly for resignation. We have a very full picture of what happened at Windsor on June 26th in a long Memorandum of the Queen's. Gladstone remained adamant although the Queen wished the ministers to remain. But Russell told her that there was an equal division in the Cabinet on the rates or rents question; that they looked to her to decide what they must do.

"It would be no use to go on with dishonour to themselves, though he admitted that Mr Gladstone had not been as conciliatory as he might have been, but that he had been very much taunted...." "The Queen called in Mr Gladstone —who looked ill and harassed...he considered Parliament dishonoured by the way in which it had treated this question now for fifteen years....He laid more stress than Lord Russell on the importance of its being a real majority of the Cabinet."[1]

A young man, a chorister at St George's, had waited at

[1] *Letters of Queen Victoria*, 2nd series, vol. i, pp. 339–342.

the railway station on this day to see the two ministers come down—and their grave faces left a lasting impression on his mind. He was, years afterwards, as Sir Frederick Bridge and Organist of Westminster Abbey, to conduct the music at Gladstone's funeral.[1] On the next day the ministry resigned.

There remained, as Bright wrote to Gladstone, "the moral force of a contest through the country". Of this important letter Morley only printed a small piece.[2] It was an attempt to "nerve Gladstone to his great duty". The Forty Thieves are, of course, the Adullamites. Bright's fear that the Tories would conspire with them "to force a reform bill which would be worse than nothing" was not justified by the events of 1867. Indeed, their leader, Lowe, was an inveterate opponent of any scheme of reform. The letter from Bright, in its entirety, reads:

BRIGHT *to* GLADSTONE

Linde Holme,
Woking.
June 24th, 1866.

56 "Dear Mr Gladstone,

I send you part of the *Manchester Examiner* of yesterday, with an article on the crisis and a report of a great meeting at Manchester. I have thought much of our last conversation and remain confirmed in my opinion that the true policy is to have a new Parliament. Resignation I only dread, or dread chiefly, in the fear that the Tory Government, if formed, might conspire with the '40 thieves' to force a Reform Bill which would be worse than nothing.

---

[1] Bridge, *A Westminster Pilgrim*, p. 47.
[2] Morley, *Life of Gladstone*, vol. I, pp. 842–3.

The 'resolution' plan I suspect must fail, though I should not be the most difficult to please. Still if definite enough to absolve you, I can hardly think it can pass except under the known alternative of dissolution.

Mr Brand makes no allowance for the moral force of a contest through the country for a great principle and a great cause. Last Easter showed how much feeling your appeals could speedily rouse. A General Election for Reform and for a Reform Government would bring an immense force of popular feeling into the field, and I do not believe in your being beaten. Besides there is something (far worse than a defeat), namely, to carry on your Government with a party poisoned and enfeebled by the baseness of the '40 traitors'.

If all the 40 came back, and if a few counties are lost, there will be gains in Ireland, and in Scotland, and in English Boroughs, and I think you would come back stronger on Reform. In great emergencies, something must be risked. You will have a great party, well compacted together and a great future. Mr Brand's figures should be forgotten for the moment.

Forgive this opinion and this advice. I think *you* are in a great crisis of your career and you must not forget the concluding passage of your great speech on the second reading of the Bill. Read it again to nerve you to your great duty.

> Believe me always,
> Sincerely yours,
> JOHN BRIGHT."

Russell, however, did appreciate the force of a contest throughout the country. In two letters to Gladstone, he paid a tribute to the enthusiasm of the great social forces, and what is more important, suggested a plan to organise them. At the moment of his passing, Russell, after a long and noble career, left a legacy to his great lieutenant and to the Liberal party. For the moment, the leader of the future was in despair; but the man who had run his race offered him counsel and advice which were to be of supreme value in the future. The successor faltered as 57 the torch was handed over. He was reminded that "the working men have stood nobly by us*" (Russell to Gladstone, July 2nd). And on July 3rd:

58 "You will observe by the enclosed paragraph which I have cut out of the *Daily News* of today, that the Conservatives of Newcastle...have had a meeting to urge the conservatives of the town 'to organise their parliamentary representation in view of the next General Election and in support of the Government of Lord Derby'. I have always supposed that the Tory Government would not give over their attempt to defeat any real reform measure without fighting a battle on the hustings. A large expenditure of money might do much in organising and preparing elections in such a manner as to produce a false instead of a bona fide representation of many towns and smaller boroughs. It seems to me that there ought to be a Liberal Association organised all over the Kingdom with a view to the next General Election, and in support of Liberal candidates. If this is practicable and expedient, I think Yorkshire and Lancashire should take the lead. But I leave the whole matter in your hands" (Russell to Gladstone).

The future was in Gladstone's hands. But we can think of no more fitting close (for such it really was) to the public life of a statesman who had always been keenly interested in reform, than the suggestion to form Liberal Associations. Throughout 1866 he had provided the inspiration; and his last thought, on relinquishing office for good, was the provision of machinery. If Gladstone was "a learner all his life", one of his wisest teachers was Lord John Russell.

Of a truth "the feeling did develop every day". On July 23rd, the railings in Hyde Park were down. Morley writing at the time said "the political stagnation ended. The crowd tore up the railings".[1] "The masses", according to Mr Dance, "knocked down the railings of Hyde Park to show they knew their mind";[2] and Northcote expected "all our heads will be broken tonight".[3] It has been easy to magnify the importance of this event; to believe (as Lowe had said earlier) that agitation had developed "into an influence of terrorism". The truth of the matter was that the affair had no elements of preparation or premeditation. But whatever the temper of the people, Gladstone remained out of the fray. In the autumn, he left for Italy, leaving the wound of the Liberal party to the healing powers of nature. But he has left us, in the shape of a letter to Sir J. Fremantle, a very valuable summary and account of his motives and actions, while he was in office in 1866. The letter explains the restraint with which he introduced the Reform Bill; and is an answer to the factious opposition which it encountered; we leave it to stand as a conclusion to this difficult chapter in Gladstone's life.

> 11, *Carlton House Terrace*,
> *June 23rd*, 1866.

"My Dear Fremantle, 59

You last night very kindly mentioned to me an impression, which had been made known to you as current among the

[1] Hirst, *Life and Letters of Lord Morley*, vol. 1, pp. 138–9.
[2] E. H. Dance, *The Victorian Illusion*, p. 43.
[3] Lang, *Stafford Northcote*, p. 161.

opposition and which you seemed to partake, that in the matter of Reform we had endeavoured to 'bully' them and that as Englishmen, they would not submit to be bullied and the like. Now this bullying must consist either in words or acts and what are they? I wish you had yourself been in the House and had seen the course of affairs and of debates and the *manner* (always excepting the front bench) of the opposite side of the House, wholly new I believe in the history of Parliament. I say this the more freely because I do not feel that individually I have anything to complain of in that respect: but what are the facts?

It is the custom in the House to refer to Lord Palmerston as a man under whom the institutions of the country were safe. Well adverting to the state of opinion and above all things determined not to be responsible for further squabbles and further discredit and disgrace to Palmerston that might arise from more miscarriages in connection with Reform, we began by cutting off in counties and towns a full third from the enfranchisement that would have been granted by our taking the figures of the very Bill that had Lord Palmerston's sanction. That was on our side *bullying the first*.

How was it met by those whose complaint you echo? By complaining that we followed the opinion of Mr Bright or as Sir H. Cairns put it, sat at his feet. Mr Bright had publicly declared that £6 and £20 were the highest franchises that would be accepted. Now as to the manner of introducing this Bill. I struggled with studious care to avoid every word that could give offence. The only use made of this was to propagate the belief that I was not in earnest and did not care for the Bill.

A great complaint was made that (anxious to increase the proprietary along with the occupation votes) we were going to swamp certain counties by the leaseholding clause. We *immediately* announced upon verifying the complaint in one single case, that we were ready to reconsider that clause.

That was *bullying the second*. Now I stop and ask what had been said or done in debate by these gentlemen who complain of being bullied? What offer had they made, what road had they opened, towards accommodation, only this a sarcastic even contemptuous recommendation to withdraw the Bill.

W. E. GLADSTONE."

(iii) *Gladstone and the Liberal Party*, 1867

It had now become obvious that the Tories were faced with a difficult task. The general belief was "that Lord Derby and his friends" would have to go much further than the ministry they had replaced. Clarendon had written prophetically to Russell on December 20th, 1865:

"I expressed my hope that the Government might produce a bill which would be generally acceptable, but that they did not mean to trifle with the question and that they would stand or fall by their measure. If it was rejected and Lord Derby came in upon opposition to reform, my fear was, I said, that instead of a moderate measure being passed quickly, a serious agitation might be created".[1]

Gladstone wrote in the same strain to Brand on October 30th, 1866: "A bill from them, to be accepted by the people, must be larger and not smaller, than would have been, or even would be, accepted from us".[2] He was absolutely convinced that the resignation in June had been in the best interests of the cause. Speaking at Ormskirk on December 19th, 1867, he recalled the events and defended his action.

[1] Gooch, *Later Correspondence of Lord John Russell*, vol. 2, p. 341.
[2] Morley, *Life of Gladstone*, vol. I, p. 856.

"We came unhesitatingly to the conclusion that the question lay between our existence as an administration on the one side, and the triumph of reform on the other. We knew perfectly well that if we retired from office, the triumph of reform was absolutely certain. We were firmly convinced that the blood of an administration would be the seed of the success of Parliamentary reform."

More serious difficulties, however, occurred in 1867, than any politician could have foreseen; and they resulted in the embarrassment of the Liberal party. The question which produced a party crisis was this: "Should it be a household suffrage cribbed, cabined and confined by the condition of personal rate-paying, or a household suffrage fairly conforming in substance and operation to the idea that the phrase conveyed. The first was in our view totally inadmissible; the second beyond the wants and wishes of the time ".[1] Gladstone believed that the exclusion of the "compounder" could be met by resolution; the schism in the Liberal party early in April made household suffrage inevitable. As soon as Disraeli laid the reform resolutions on the table, great activity began among the Liberals, 289 of them meeting in Gladstone's house. We have three accounts of this meeting, and two of them are of considerable value. The first from C. P. Villiers to Delane offers a striking contrast to the later "Tea Room" desertion. " I have not seen such unanimity in trusting to one man's (Gladstone's) lead for these thirty years. He has got an immense hold now over the party, and they came today ready to adopt whatever he proposed "[2] (February 26th,

[1] Morley, *Life of Gladstone*, vol. I, pp. 857–60.
[2] Dasent, *Life of Delane*, vol. II, p. 190.

1867). "Gladstone", wrote Brand, "opened the proceedings, pressing for union amongst the Liberal party with a view to a satisfactory settlement of Reform, and setting aside considerations of office."[1] But this first meeting was, in a sense, artificial; and all three accounts agree that little could be done until the Government moved. The crisis came when they met a month later. In the meantime, Disraeli had begun that series of moves which have generally been interpreted as the outcome of a cynical disregard of principles. Roundell Palmer, a man not given to suffering the unscrupulous gladly, however, took a different view. The Conservatives were not merely dishonest. "If substance were regarded, Mr Disraeli and his friends were as much entitled as anybody else to take advantage of their tenure of power to settle, if they could, a critical question which could not remain where it was and which if they left it alone, would be made the battle ground against them."[2] The battle started, a grave problem confronted Gladstone. Should he fight, if any principle seemed at stake, or should he acquiesce? On one question Lowe urged resistance—the principle of fighting rent against rating. He wrote to Gladstone on March 21st, 1867, a long and stimulating letter. Morley quoted only a fragment;[3] indeed, this part of his narrative is brief; he seems to have wanted to hurry over a dark chapter to the more congenial topic of the next one—the Irish Church. His only documents, at this stage, are extracts from diaries.

[1] Dasent, *Life of Delane*, vol. II, p. 191.
[2] Selborne, *Memorials*, 2nd series, vol. I, p. 63.
[3] Morley, *Life of Gladstone*, vol. I, p. 865.

Lowe appears to have been unaware of Gladstone's real position; though there existed "a disinclination", events proved his contention to be completely untrue that "if you only stand firm you are master of the position". Gladstone wished to stand firm; and this resolve, challenged first by the party, robbed him of any control of the situation. Possibly the Liberal meeting of February 26th explained his hope. We quote the complete letter.

34, *Lowndes Square*,
March 21st, 1867.

60 "My dear Gladstone,

The crisis at which we have arrived and my own total absence from any party or personal interest must excuse me for writing to you. I need not waste time in shewing how necessary it is to rid the country of the present ministry, nor how important it is, if possible, to stop their bill before the second reading. They are by the contagion of their own immorality breaking up and demoralising everything around them and their bill if once read a second time will have acquired a momentum most difficult to arrest and which will I fear carry them into committee. I do not dwell on these things for I am sure they must strike you as they do me, nor yet on the great peril of a division on the Borough Franchise clause taken under the threat of a dissolution and the pressure of the radical members of constituencies. Neither need I enlarge to you on the position in which you will be placed if after having so eloquently and vehemently dissected and destroyed its principle, you are driven to allow the second reading to pass without a division—you may after such a check remain the nominal leader of the Liberals but Ichabod, the glory is departed—the more complete your success on Monday last, the more signal your failure on Monday next if your party will not support you in following up your blow. The Tory policy has been to break up the discipline of party by placing themselves in advance of the Liberals. They are content to dislocate their own party if they can only disorganise their antagonists. There never was a time when a leader was more needed, and when it was more absolutely necessary to support authority and enforce obedience. I am told that you are anxious to oppose the second reading and that there is a disinclination in the party to join in the attack. I believe they are not more indispensable to you than you to them and that if you only stand firm you are master of the position. They have no other possible leader than you at the present time—you possess in a great measure the confidence of the ultras and of the moderates, in a measure certainly to which no one else can make any pretension. I have just seen Cranbourne who believes that he can bring you a good many Tories to resist the second reading. I need not say that you may count on all the little influence I can exert and all the help I can give—*Horsman* is quite of the same mind. My object in writing to you is to press you most earnestly to stand firm and not to allow yourself to be turned aside by any threat of defection, or any apprehension of failure. This is one of those occasions in life when it is worth while to stake high and play boldly. If you succeed you have saved us from a great danger and confirmed your position as leader, if you fail you are scarcely worse off than you will be if notoriously forced to abandon your ground and to assent to that very principle which you have demolished. They cannot do without you, they have no other leader to look to—you are really far more independent of them than they of you. Take a decided and confident tone at your meeting tomorrow and I feel convinced the threatened disaffection will die away. Since Callimachus the Polemarch at Marathon no one had a weightier cause to decide. It is vain to say the principle of the Bill is lowering the Franchise—the principle is rating as opposed to rent and any attempt in Committee to put back any figure of rent will be met by the greatest obstacles when the principle is once conceded.

I would further suggest that if anything can be gained by it nothing is more reasonable than to ask for delay. The Franchise is now quite unknown and undiscussed by the Press and not understood perfectly even by Disraeli himself.

Pray excuse the liberty I have taken in urging these things on you. Shall it be said that Disraeli has such an influence that he can lead his followers where he will (and that is generally to ruin) and that you cannot take upon yourself authority to lead them against an enemy whom they have every reason to distrust and despise.

Believe me always,

Very truly yours,

R. LOWE."

On the day that Lowe wrote this letter another meeting of the Liberal party, very different in temper from the previous one, was held again (March 21st). (This, the second one, Morley alone mentions.[1]) The best account of it is in the Queen's letters.[2]

"At the meeting of the Liberal party to-day, Mr Gladstone addressed them and gave twelve reasons why the Bill should be thrown out on the second reading. The moment he mentioned this, there was a murmur and scuffling of feet. He started, but continued his address, and spoke with great energy and emphasis, concluding that there never was anything more clear for a party, than their duty and interest to vote against the second reading. There was revived the same murmur of dissent and disapprobation, and cries of 'Bright'. ...The cries renewed....Mr Bright came forward. He

[1] Morley, *Life of Gladstone*, vol. I, p. 866.
[2] Disraeli to Queen Victoria, 21st March. *Letters of Queen Victoria*, 2nd series, vol. I, p. 412.

supported Mr Gladstone with great fire and fervour.... All this is from an eye-witness and may be depended upon. It comes to this: if the Cabinet will be wise 'it must take' a bold stand on *personal rating*."

Gladstone's device would have drawn a line below which houses should not be rated at all; but he remained firm, that the payment of rates, under any system, carried a vote with it. He was not in favour, then, of household suffrage pure and simple; and, in this opinion, he came near to Bright who feared that danger would result from admitting the "residuum" of the community. We have three estimates of Gladstone's position at the end of this meeting (on the question of opposing the second reading of Disraeli's Reform Bill). Morley says he "concurred" (to refrain from opposing) "not over willingly".[1] "Gladstone acquiesced...I think, not willingly, but there was no real choice."[2] "Gladstone acquiesced 'readily'."[3] At all events, a group of Liberals came to the conclusion that they could give Gladstone's device no support; they would not have rated and unrated. Gladstone fought for the principle that payment of rates in any form should merit the privilege; but he was no longer "master of the situation" and a mutiny broke out. No one could have been more staggered than he, when he discovered that the rejection of his plan led directly to the abolition of compounding.

For the moment, despair settled on the brow of the leader. "In the singular mental condition of our party

[1] Morley, *Life of Gladstone*, vol. 1, p. 866.
[2] Lord Selborne's *Memorials*, 2nd series, vol. 1, pp. 68-9.
[3] Trevelyan, *Life of Bright*, p. 372.

it may be well that I should lie by for a little while "[1] (March 27th, 1867). Ten days before the Tea Room split:

"I can hardly speak a word in the Commons, especially if it in any manner oppose or reflect on Disraeli, with any confidence that some man will not rise on the Liberal side to protest against it. It is an almost unexampled position— a party of vast strength is completely paralysed by internal dissension. But for myself I think the best course is to avoid all acts of leadership which can be dispensed with ".[1]

One great man, however, remained by his side. We have two more letters from Bright; one on the question of rates (May 11th) before the motion of Mr Hodgkinson, May 27th, abolished compounding in parliamentary boroughs, and put this part of the subject *hors de combat*. The second is in the style Bright could employ so pungently on his best friends when roused.

At the close of 1867 we leave the Liberal party in confusion, and its leader baffled, not by any problem, but by the incredible machinations of men. A new dawn came with the Irish Question; the party rallied. It was not to fall away again until the 'eighties; and then, Ireland, which had been the unifying force, caused the dismemberment.

BRIGHT *to* GLADSTONE

4, *Hanover Street*,
May 11th, 1867.

61 "Dear Mr Gladstone,

I have been considering a mode of getting out of the

---

[1] Gooch, *Later Correspondence of Lord John Russell*, vol. 2, p. 359.

difficulty created by the late division, and wish to submit it to you. I take two towns to illustrate the difficulty and the remedy. In Rochdale there is no Small Tenements Act and no Compounding Act, but generally through the town, the landlord or owners of cottages pay the rates and are repaid in the rents charged to the occupiers. The occupiers names are on the rate book, *the full sum of the rate is paid*, by tenant or owners, as the case may be, and the Franchise is preserved in Rochdale. The vote will be 'Household', and yet the *occupier* will have all the advantages of the system of compounding. In Birmingham, there is no Small Tenements Act, but there are Compounding Acts, all of which goes up to Houses rated as high as £12 or about £16 rental. The *full rate* is not paid, and the occupiers generally are not entered on the Rate book, excepting those who have been enfranchised under the 3rd section of Clay's Act, and who are now to be disenfranchised. What is wanted is, not to disturb the plan of paying the Rate of the landlord, but to abolish the 'composition' or the payment of the reduced rate, so that the occupier would have still the advantages of the system of compounding. His name being on the Rate book and *his full rate paid*, whether by himself or his landlord, he would appear on the Register of Voters.

Under this plan, the payment by the owner would be voluntary as in Rochdale. He would get no allowance from the Parish and *he would not pay for empty houses*. But he would undertake the payment as a convenience to his Tenants, and he would have no difficulty in repaying himself for the small difference by an addition of 3*d*. per week or some such sum, which would probably be ample for him, seeing that he would not be required to pay for empty houses. In cases where the owner from any cause was unwilling to continue to pay the Rate, the occupier would be obliged to do it, but I believe the advantages to him of *paying everything in his rent* would be so great, that owners willing to pay would find their houses sought after and in demand by the working men, and that the payment by the owner would still prevail.

I propose: that our great lawyer should consider this case, and if it is thought a reasonable one, that he should prepare a short bill for immediate introduction to Parliament with a view of passing it alongside this 'Reform Bill' and so to extend to all the Boroughs the franchise which is to be given by it to the 29 favoured Boroughs.

The Bill should repeal all the powers given by existing acts to make *allowance to Landlords* who undertake to pay the Rate, on condition that they pay for houses whether full or empty. It should leave parishes and owners the power to arrange for payment by the owners, but *of the full rate only*, and thus abolish the 'composition' or reduced and disenfranchising rate.

I think in such a Bill it might be well to draw a line as in Scotland, and to exempt Houses under £4 value from it, leaving the power of composition to the owners of them as at present with some limit, say half the rate, for the allowance to be made by the Parish. I do not think this important, but it would adopt the Scotch and Irish system almost exactly and this would be an argument for it in the House.

I believe that out of the 245,000 occupiers whose full rate is now paid, and who are to be enfranchised, that a very large number of them pay their rates through their landlord, and that the 'personal' payment by them directly to the overseers does not take place. This is true of Rochdale, as I have learned this morning from our Liberal agent there, and I believe it is true of many and perhaps of most other towns.

I may be wrong in this, but I believe I have suggested a mode of overcoming our great difficulty. There will be little trouble in making it work. Every occupier will see the reasonableness of some *small increase* of rent to meet the increased rate paid by the landlord. It will be very small, perhaps it ought to be none at all, as the owner will save something by no longer paying for empty houses, and *he will have the compensation of obtaining his rate.*

If this plan were offered to the working men occupiers of houses in all the Boroughs, I am sure it would be accepted with enthusiasm and the owners as a class could make no opposition to it, and very many of them would adopt it as a wise arrangement of a great difficulty.

I wish you would carefully consider this proposition. If it is sound, I would have a Bill drawn at once and endeavour to carry it through this session. All the existing political machinery for agitation would help it forward, and we might possibly catch some men too clever by half in their own trap, and end a great question by establishing equal justice in the giving of the franchise throughout all the Boroughs of England and Wales.

Asking your early and careful consideration of this—I am,

Always most sincerely yours,

JOHN BRIGHT."

BRIGHT *to* GLADSTONE

Rochdale,
July 31*st,* 1867.

"Dear Mr Gladstone,   62

I am amazed at the course taken by Lord Russell and his friends on the vote for two members only where a Borough returns three.

It is an astounding proposition that 'London' henceforth is to have *two voices* in any great division, and that Liverpool, Manchester, Birmingham and Leeds are to have only *one voice* or vote each, and that this is to be brought about by the votes of professing Liberal Peers given against Lord Derby's Government and Bill.

I have done all I can to support Lord Russell last year and this, and I think it hard after fighting for years with his opponents and our own, to be dealt a more grievous blow by him than any I have received from them.

I would rather see the whole Bill abandoned than have this odious proposition accepted. It is a strange course for a reforming Peer and Statesman to carry via Lord Derby a clause proposed by *Lord Cairns* to reduce London to the voting power of Tamworth, and the other great Boroughs to the condition of Arundel and Colne.

Glasgow is to have three members but on the ancient and right principle. One is to be given to South Glasgow, and no 'majority' will be destroyed. Why are the other great Boroughs to be treated in a different manner?

I am happy to know that you have not sanctioned this scheme, but Lord Russell. Sir George Grey and Mr Cardwell have—and I suppose other Whig Peers have gone with Lord Russell. I cannot express the amazement and disgust with which I have seen the course they have taken, and I can only see increased disaster to the Liberal party from leadership so imbecile and so ruinous. I can keep no terms with 'Liberal' Statesmen who are ready thus to treat great constituencies of the Kingdom.

The men on our own side who object to bring Lord Russell back to office and who complain of some of your friends are justified by this unhappy vote. I must hold myself free from any party combination, rather than be understood to fight alongside men who know so little what is due to the principles of their party. Imbecility or treachery is fatal to success. We have seen the treachery all through the session, and now we witness the imbecility. Forgive this note. You may say I am more angry than wise, it may be so—but I cannot help telling you what I think and feel. I am certain you must regret what has been done. I discussed this matter with Lord Russell on Thursday, being most anxious he should not go wrong. I could not tell him all I thought about it, and now I prefer to write to you rather than to him.

The whole course of the Whig Peers seems to me childish and absurd, and they are playing into the hands of Lord Derby at the next election.

This is of importance to you who should have a great future in the English Parliament. To me it is a great grief because I have always hoped that the best of the peerage would go with the people.

I can keep my spirits up under the severest blows of our adversaries, but I am ready to sink under the pressure of the feebleness of those who have been supposed to be our friends.

I hope Mr Disraeli will be more true to the great Boroughs than Lord Russell has been. A few days will show.

Believe me,

Faithfully yours,

JOHN BRIGHT."

CHAPTER IX

THE RESOLUTIONS ON THE IRISH CHURCH AND THE GENERAL ELECTION OF 1868

"He is much more likely to become a democratic leader now that he sits for a big town."

Charles Dilke.

THE last great question which occupied Gladstone in the 'sixties was the question of the Protestant Establishment in Ireland. For the purpose of this study, it is the climax. We separate both the Resolutions and the Bill from the general work of Gladstone's first ministry, because it represents the final expression of his policy in the most critical ten years of his life, and because it heralds the supreme struggle and major occupation of his years as a Prime Minister. In tracing the rise of Gladstone to the leadership of the Liberal party, we reach in his policy towards the Irish Church the last stage of a development and the first stage of a maturity. In our period, it is the crowning example of a courage which had been facing and meeting unpalatable questions since 1859.

We have to admit that, in this case, the incubation period had been extremely short. Northcote wrote on March 29th, 1865, "Gladstone made a terribly long stride in his downward progress last night and denounced the Irish Church in a way which shows how, by-and-by, he will deal not only with it but with the Church of

England too. I wonder how *The Guardian* will get over it, and what Palmer thought of him ".[1] (This was prophetic, at least, as far as it concerned Roundell Palmer's fears in 1868–9. The *Memorials* reveal his keen anxiety, on purely logical grounds, for the Church of England.) But whatever he thought in 1865, Gladstone believed in 1866 that there was no urgency. "In meeting a question with a negative" (a motion against the Irish Church) "we may always put it on the ground of time, as well as on the merits" (April 7th, 1866).[2] A new and startling succession of events soon provided the "ground of time"; in 1867 a succession of Fenian outrages, notably at Manchester and at Clerkenwell, startled the English public.

"When the metropolis itself was shocked and horrified by an inhuman outrage, when a sense of insecurity went abroad far and wide...then it was when these phenomena came home to the popular mind, and produced that attitude of attention and preparedness on the part of the whole population of this country which qualified them to embrace, in a manner foreign to their habits in other times, the vast importance of the Irish controversy."

This was Gladstone's *casus belli*.[3] This declaration merits careful attention, because men charged him afterwards with diagnosing the malady but prescribing the wrong medicine. The Fenians, they said in effect, did not commit their outrages to emphasise the ecclesiastical anomalies in Ireland. Why then proceed to reform the

[1] Lang, *Stafford Northcote*, p. 135.
[2] Morley, *Life of Gladstone*, vol. I, p. 873.
[3] *Ibid.* vol. I, p. 876.

Church? Gladstone replied decisively to this objection in the great speech of March 23rd, 1869.

"The right honourable gentleman (Mr Gathorne Hardy) reminds us that the Fenians have not asked for the abolition of the Church in Ireland....The Fenians...are the very last persons to demand its abolition, because it serves their purpose that it should remain as it now stands. Whatever serves to estrange the minds of the Irish population from Imperial rule, is of all things the most precious part of the Fenian stock-in-trade, and it would ill suit their purpose indeed to ask to have the Church in Ireland abolished."

This was the statesman's answer; he had discovered the truth in what was *not* asked. With these views, he could have no time for Disraeli's plan of "levelling up". "Root and branch" must be the cry. "I say we are justified in saying that the time has come when every man standing on this floor is entitled and bound to say that what is called the reform of the Church of Ireland, by cutting and clipping and paring, by taking away a little here, and putting in a little there, has become utterly hopeless."[1]

He raised his standard at Southport on December 9th, 1867. In returning thanks for his election he said "Two years and a half ago, you found me a stranded man" (*in forma pauperis* again). Then he went on "I would not for a moment listen to any plea whatever for separate institutions and a separate policy for England or for Scotland or for Ireland". Yet "You must be prepared for a course of long and patient well doing towards Ireland". On the same day he had received a letter from Bright, who had made a life-long study of what was for

[1] Speech, March 23rd, 1869.

him "the land of evictions". Twenty years before he had thundered against those who laid the calamities of Ireland at the door of providence; those who in Cornewall Lewis's words "altogether despair of establishing permanent tranquillity in Ireland and who think that it is an exception to all the ordinary rules of government". Bright had insisted all along that "we must do our part—we must retrace our steps—we must shun the blunders". Though his solution was "We must free the land" (1849), he wrote to Gladstone on the question of the hour—the Church.

BRIGHT *to* GLADSTONE

Rochdale.
December 9th, 1867.

"Dear Mr Gladstone,

63

I send the letter[1] on the Irish Church which I mentioned to you. It was written 15 years ago, and soon after a visit I had paid to Ireland. On reading it again at this distance of time, I have nothing to retract or change in it. I believe such a scheme as that propounded in it, would meet with more support and less opposition than any other scheme which professes to establish the voluntary Church system in Ireland, and any plan, to be of use, must get rid of the State Church system in that country.

I shall be glad if you will read this letter over carefully, and before you condemn it, I must ask you to read it over twice. This is not from egotism, but because I have given much consideration to this question, and from a standpoint very different from yours, but one from which it must be looked at by any Statesman who undertakes to grapple with it.

I see that Mr Hunt is gone to Ireland and probably the Government will try some new job, akin to the Galway

[1] Quoted in Trevelyan's *Life of Bright,* pp. 167–9.

packet job in the hope of getting Irish votes. I think they cannot undertake to settle the Church or any Land question during the coming Session.

I will thank you to return the inclosed.

> I am always,
>> Faithfully yours,
>>> JOHN BRIGHT."

Gladstone replied:

> *Hawarden Castle.*
> *December 10th, 1867.*

64 "My dear Mr Bright,

I return your able and interesting letter. I think you have supposed the existence of some prejudice in my mind against your plans, which does not really dwell there. This is no new affair with me. I started in life a believer in the Irish Church establishment, and I spoke strongly for it more than 30 years ago. But in 1845 when I left office to place myself in a position of freedom with respect to Sir Robert Peel's proposal on the Maynooth grant, I considered that I became free with respect to all Irish Ecclesiastical questions, and on first standing for Oxford in 1847, I declined pledging myself in principle to the Irish Established Church. If I took long to ruminate upon the matter before speaking, it was first because in Ireland itself the question slept; and secondly because it is well to ponder much upon a subject that if I mistake not, will prove very difficult to deal with, and may again lead the Liberal party to martyrdom. My own personal difficulties or preferences on this great matter are as nothing to me, compared with the evil of the present system and the advantage of altering it fundamentally. Further I think that it is better so to alter it, as to destroy the principle of State Establishment in Ireland, better for the country at large, better for the members of the body itself, although I regret from another point of view, to do anything which by removing certain Bishops from the House of Lords affects the constitution of that house and weakens what is in one sense a popular element in its composition. The basis of your plan seems to me the best of any I have seen in print. There are many details that in your outline you have not mentioned and which would require time to consider; but the basis is the main thing.

Meantime a letter I have received this morning warns me that the Liberal Farmers about Ormskirk (whither I go next week) are for maintaining the Irish Church in its integrity!

I remain,

Sincerely yours,

W. E. GLADSTONE."

This is an interesting chapter of autobiography and prophecy. South Lancashire rejected him on the question because Protestantism which believed in an establishment was strong there. But the phrase most to our purpose is "it is well to ponder much"—yet another example of a long process of thought coming to fruition and being translated into action. This is an effective answer to Mr Dance's contention. "The Liberals", he says, "were compelled to cast about in a hurry for something upon which to oppose the Conservatives, and Gladstone's mind, moving as usual in its mysterious way, discovered the urgency of the Irish Church question."[1] How dangerous was the stratagem that might "lead the Liberal party to martyrdom"! And can any instance be quoted, in Gladstone's sixty years of public life, when he espoused a great cause for the mere purpose of dishing the enemy? Again, says Mr Dance,

[1] E. H. Dance, *The Victorian Illusion*, pp. 103–4.

"It is probable that he approved of something like disestablishment at the time of his resignation over the Maynooth grant twenty years previously" (the letter makes it *certain* that he became free to "ruminate") "and it is certain that not many months before he launched disestablishment upon an unwilling Queen and an unwilling Parliament, he had declared quite definitely his belief that it was well outside the politics of the day".[1]

Morley has explained the reason why Gladstone said in 1865 that "the question was remote". He felt that his own political life was drawing to a close.[2] In a very short time, however, he became convinced that the hour had come when Irish grievances demanded attention. "I have been watching the sky with a strong sense of the obligation to act with the first streak of dawn."

With the dawn of 1868, Fenianism had brought the question into practical politics. The old policy of a succession of Coercion Bills would no longer do. It was an anxious time for the Liberal party, which had not yet recovered from the confusion of 1867.

65 "Do you not think", wrote Childers[3] to Gladstone on January 15th, 1868, "that it might be well to get together, before we meet, some of the leading *honest* Liberals, and to discuss the two or three questions as to which uniform action is so desirable? For instance, as to the rating clauses, the Scotch Additions, education and the Irish Land question, we are all very much adrift. I do not think that such a meeting should be confined to ex-officials."

The year 1868 is of great importance in the history of the Liberal party, not only because it foreshadows the

[1] E. H. Dance, *The Victorian Illusion*, p. 104.
[2] Morley, *Life of Gladstone*, vol. 1, p. 874.   [3] H. C. E. Childers.

work of Gladstone's First Ministry, but because the Irish Question, which divided the party in the end, would wait no longer. Another break with the past gave a new character to the time also. Disraeli became Prime Minister in February, with the certain conviction that his antagonist was about to make another serious blunder.

"Mr Disraeli cannot conceal from himself that we are embarking on stormy waters, and that a very serious political season is setting in....He thinks that Mr Gladstone has mistaken the spirit of the times and the temper of the country. The abhorrence of Popery, the dread of Ritualism, and the hatred of the Irish, have long been smouldering in the mind of the nation. They will seize, Mr Disraeli thinks, the opportunity long sighed for and now offered, to vent their accumulated passion."[1]

Stormy times were indeed coming; and though "the accumulated (or better still *fostered*) passion" defeated Gladstone in South Lancashire, Disraeli's prophecy was destined not to be fulfilled. The issues were serious and the portents grave. "Many Liberals were profoundly disaffected to their leader. To attack the Irish Church was to alarm and scandalise his own chosen friends and closest allies in the kindred Church of England." The No-popery cry, the inevitable hostility of the Lords and the "legislative task", combined to make the problem "gigantic".[2] Gladstone, however, did not shrink. "The time had come", he said in March, "when the Church of Ireland as a Church in alliance with the state must

[1] To Queen Victoria, March 23. *Letters of Queen Victoria*, 2nd series, vol. I, p. 517.
[2] Morley, *Life of Gladstone*, vol. I, p. 880.

cease to exist." In this spirit, he proceeded to frame and to present the four celebrated resolutions of April and May. The evil upas tree must cause no more blight. Before the question went to the country, in one of Gladstone's greatest election campaigns, he came into conflict with the Queen and with the House of Lords. The resolutions were carried, but the third aroused great controversy; it proposed that an address be presented to Her Majesty praying that "...H.M. would be pleased to place at the disposal of Parliament her interest in the temporalities of the Irish Church". The newspapers interpreted this to mean that Gladstone intended to cause the Queen to leave unfulfilled duties imposed upon her by the Constitution and recognised by her in the Coronation oath. Granville sought to appease the Queen by a detailed statement of the true facts.[1] But the conclusive answer came from Gladstone, a year later, when introducing the bill (March 23rd, 1869).

"It is the greatest mistake to suppose that since the Reformation, the Royal supremacy has always been flowing, as it were, through the same channel...but as long as the Queen is supreme in every cause that can be brought into a court for the purpose whether of primary adjudication or of review, so long the Royal supremacy exists. If any one be prepared to question that doctrine, I ask them whether the Royal supremacy exists in Scotland at this moment or not?"

The first act closed when the Lords threw out the bill suspending for the meantime any movements within the Church of Ireland. With the resignation of Disraeli, the

[1] Fitzmaurice, *Life of Granville*, vol. I, pp. 523–5.

question was taken to the country, and a great election campaign immediately began. We have an interesting letter of May 22nd from W. E. Forster, who wrote to advise Gladstone on the probable tactics of the opposition, and on the question whether the old constituencies must bind the new ones. A definite plan of action, he said, would lead to an appeal to the old; an abstract resolution would postpone the issue.

> 80, *Eccleston Square,*
> *London, S.W.*
> *Sunday, March 22nd,* 1868.

"Dear Mr Gladstone, **66**

At the risk of telling you what you already know, I think I ought to send you some information I have heard, and on which I am disposed to rely, respecting Disraeli's probable tactics. Partly from a passage in your speech, and partly from a paragraph in the *Star*, your intention to move an address for the stoppage of appointments is suspected, and I am told that while Disraeli would meet an abstract resolution against the Irish Church by saying that, if beaten, he would neither resign nor dissolve *now*, but would appeal as soon as possible to the new constituencies—yet, that he would meet a 'stoppage' address with a threat of instant dissolution, alleging that he would be *forced* to ask the present constituencies *whether they wish thus to bind the future constituencies*. I am also told that upon this issue we have much defection and may be met by a cross motion to the effect that the moribund constituencies ought not to bind by any act the new constituencies.

What with selfish fear of dissolution, and what with dislike of the odium of supporting a move which would be said to force on a premature dissolution which would be generally unpopular, I think it probable that such cross motion might succeed. While, however, I think you ought to be prepared for the probability of defeat, I shall not myself regret the moving of the stoppage address, because I think it would give us a clear and good issue for the new constituencies, and I care little what success Disraeli gets with the present Parliament. But may I venture to suggest whether it might not be well to divide the motion by proposing as it were two motions:

(1) a resolution that the Irish Church should cease as an establishment;
(2) that the Queen be requested to make no further appointments.

If we took this course, I think we must carry No. 1; that anyway would be a great gain.

Apologising for thus intruding on you reasons which you may have considered, and suggestions which may be worthless.

> I am,
>> Yours faithfully,
>>> W. E. FORSTER."

The appeal was to be made then to the old constituencies. In the autumn and winter Gladstone worked unceasingly in South Lancashire; speaking at every important town and borough. The campaign had an entirely modern character; constituencies were intensively worked. It was the direct precursor of Midlothian and the election that we know. Beginning at St Helens in August, Gladstone's constant note remained: " Ireland can wait no longer. Now that you have the power, refuse any adjournment. It is the institutions of Ireland which cause discontent. Do not wait to continue from year to year the painful—the ignominious, I would almost say, the loathsome—process of suspending personal liberty in order to keep large portions of the Irish people down by force". He recalled to his audience Lytton's phrase: "We talk of 'Irish Bulls'; but the words 'Irish Church' are the greatest bull in the language". And he went on

"If Ireland is at this moment a grief, in many respects, a scandal, and in possible cases a danger to this Empire—the blame of that retrospectively may be thrown upon others, by whom in other times you and your forefathers have been governed. It can no longer—if it continue—be so lightly and easily discharged from you now that you are invested with the privileges by which you are to govern yourselves".[1]

It is on the strength of the closing sentence, that we regard the election of 1868 as the first of a new series: Gladstone swept through the long chain of ugly manufacturing towns; Widnes, Warrington, Newton, Leigh, with one refrain: "The Church of Ireland is the Church of a minority, insignificant in numbers, great in property, in education and in power. All this does not amend, but aggravates the case. For if a National Church be not the Church of the nation, it should at least be the Church of the poor".[2] He came at length to the Mersey.

"I wish I had been with you [i.e. the Liberals] much sooner", he said at Bootle, "I hope nothing will induce me to recede from the soil upon which I was born. This Bootle, gentlemen, which we now see covered with the houses of thinking citizens, I remember it a wilderness of sandhills with its grouse and wild roses. What has changed it? In no

---

[1] St Helens, August 5th, *Speeches in South-west Lancashire*, 1868.
[2] Foreword, *South Lancashire Speeches*, 1868.

small part, the beneficent legislation which has struck the fetters from the arms of human industry."

But defeat was at hand. Odious charges had been brought against him; among the seafaring men in particular, the voice of calumny had been busy. He repudiated with warmth the charge that he was "a Jesuit in disguise" at Garston, then a small village, a few miles south of Liverpool.[1] On November 23rd, he faced the inhabitants of the capital of South Lancashire for the last time, as a candidate. He had made many great speeches here: he would make many triumphal progresses through the streets in the future. Though the borough of Liverpool remained loyal, he lost the battle and never again sat in Parliament as its member. The morning of nomination dawned wet and raw; Gladstone faced a huge crowd on the hustings set up in Lime Street. Times had changed since Canning spoke from the window in Rodney Street, in that quiet and dignified neighbourhood which still remains remote from the noise of the modern world. The very centre of political power had shifted from such an area, to the bustling commercial streets lower in the town. Behind Gladstone, in the mist, loomed up that tremendous hall, a monument to the new spirit of municipal enterprise, which had been built since Canning's day. In front of him, further evidence of the changing world—the scaffolding of the new railway hotel, on which the more vociferous members of the crowd perched. Between these two great reminders of the power of the urban community and of the joint stock company, he could not have helped feeling that the days

[1] *Liverpool Mercury*, November 16th, 1868.

of privilege and of sheltered institutions, had passed by. "Go back to Oxford", shouted some daring spirits. But Gladstone never turned back; as the member for Greenwich, he applied himself with renewed vigour to the task of reform. One characteristic of the election we cannot ignore; Gladstone's reiterated warning that expenditure must be checked. "The rapid growth of wealth, especially among the classes of the greatest activity and enterprise has led, for a number of years past, to a diminished watchfulness outside the walls of Parliament respecting the great and cardinal subject of economy in the public charges and the relation between the income of the state and its expenditure."[1] At Leigh, in particular, his warning was grave and impressive; and he concluded "I hope that the greatest caution will ever be exercised by the labouring classes with regard to the management of joint stock enterprise". The election, then, not only foretold the interest of the Liberals in Ireland, but also their interest in economy and balanced budgets.

We conclude our survey of the year 1868, with two letters. The first, from the Marquis of Hartington, gives us another glimpse of the altered character of a general election, and speaks for itself. (It is interesting to note that the wives and daughters of the operatives attended the Leigh meeting.) The second, from Bright, deals with the future. It is the programme of the first Liberal ministry. But ministers and bills and Parliament were secondary to the new and all-important force: "the people will go for these things".

[1] Foreword, *South Lancashire Speeches*, 1868.

Hardwick Hall,
Chesterfield.
October 1st, 1868.

67 "My dear Mr Gladstone,

You have received or will receive a request from Preston to take part in the proceedings of an 'aggregate tea meeting' to be held about the 11th of this month. I have been asked to support the request, and I do so to the extent of assuring you that your presence there would of course be of great use both to the Liberal Borough Candidates and to me. I have, however, told the promoters that with your own canvass before you it is not reasonable to expect that you can comply. Some of my Committee have, however, suggested, though not in a definite shape, that it might be of immense use, if on some day nearer to the election, when you have finished your own canvass, and when the concession could not be made an excuse for fresh requests from other places, you could address a public meeting at Preston.

The large number of your own constituents who live in the two Northern Divisions would give a sufficient ground for your appearance at Preston, the most central place in the North; and I have no doubt that such a meeting would do us all a great deal of good.

I remain,

Yours very Sincerely,

HARTINGTON."

Private.

Rochdale.
November 27th, 1868.

68 "My dear Mr Gladstone,

I have sent you a copy of my speeches spoken during the recent election at Birmingham,—to one of them only am I wishful to call your attention. It is the one at page 41 of the pamphlet, and refers to the subject of public or national Education. It met with a most hearty response from all my friends in Birmingham who heard it or read it. This question will not wait long for a settlement, and what we have just seen in this County and its boroughs makes me the more anxious about it. It is a question which will appeal more forcibly to the new borough constituencies than any other, and a Liberal Administration will be compelled to deal with it.

I am surprised that you came so near winning in your County Contest for I did not expect it. The extension of our boroughs, and the shutting out from the County of the Leaseholders in boroughs has thrown this Division into the Tory ranks. Almost all the land, and almost all who occupy it, are the 'property' of men of Tory principles and prejudices, and 'tho' one rose from the dead', I should have no hope that these occupiers with open voting could give their votes in opposition to those who rule over them.

I consider the Ballot as needful and inevitable as a wider suffrage was two years ago. Throughout the Liberal ranks (I speak of men just elected) it has made great progress as you will have seen, and I am pretty sure that a majority of the new House is pledged to it. For a Liberal Government to follow the unwise course of Lord Grey's Government after 1832, and to resist it, will be the beginning of weakness in the party, and will end in difficulty and perhaps in its destruction.

The corruption, bribery, compulsion and tumult of this general election have probably never been exceeded—the whole country is disgraced, and it ought to be shocked, and no man *who has no other remedy to offer* can with any show of reason resist the Ballot. I should like to have an earnest enquiry into the whole matter and manner of our elections in the hope that some complete remedy may be found. With our now large constituencies the machinery of our elections requires review. The barbarous system of open nominations and open voting should be abolished.

In my view of the future there is plenty of work for you.

173

The Irish Church—a fight with the 'Services' for a less expenditure—the secret or free vote—and a scheme for education. The people will go for these things. They are worth everything to them and the Tory party can neither adopt nor successfully resist them.

Forgive this troublesome note. If you do not agree with me, it will do you no harm to know what I am thinking about.

I am always,

Sincerely yours,

JOHN BRIGHT."

P.S. This needs no answer—it is too near the 10th December to enter into correspondence.

In 1869, Gladstone introduced the Irish Church Bill, as Prime Minister for the first time. He "descended the hill of life", but "he ascended a steepening path with a burden ever gathering in weight".[1] One part of this great episode in his career only concerns us: that is the policy urged by Bright of mastering and settling the Irish land problem. He recognised in Gladstone a man who had the cause of Ireland sincerely at heart. Speaking in the House of Commons in April, 1866, he had said: "He (the Chancellor of the Exchequer) is the only man of this Government whom I have heard of late years who has spoken as if he comprehended this question.... I should like to ask him whether this Irish Question is above the stature of himself and of his colleagues?" Bright did feel that they shrank from considering the Irish Question as a whole; and he wrote, in a different strain to a friend in Ireland on January 27th, 1868: "Mr Gladstone hesitates and hardly knows how far to

[1] Diary, December 29th, 1868.

174

go. The material of his forces is not good, and I suspect he has not studied the land question, and knows little about it ".[1] It was in this spirit that he wrote to Gladstone in the summer of 1869, urging that the burning question had been shelved. It was largely through his persistence that the Liberal ministry proceeded in 1870, to the complementary, and as he felt, more important question.

Private.   *Rochdale.*
                                          July 30*th*, 1869.

   " I suggested[2] to you that some one should go to Berlin to 69 report on the Prussian Land system and their ' Rent Banks '.

   Would Sir L. Mallett be the right man?[3] When the Lords drew back on the Irish Church Bill, they avoided a deep hole —they were on the brink of it and were only just saved.

   The Irish Church would have been almost forgotten, in the greater question that would have been raised. I am glad that greater is, at least, postponed. I feel as if I were becoming too old and heavy to wish for more great Questions.

   The Irish Land, the Ballot and a good broad Education Bill—all carried through Parliament—then I could be content to stay at home, and look on at my successors in the political field " (Bright to Gladstone).

The Irish Question helps us to an understanding of one of Gladstone's greatest qualities. It reveals, perhaps better than any other public work, the processes by which he translated thought into action. His moral sense drove many subjects beneath his eye; his intellect grappled with them; but it was his heart (as Cobden

---

[1] O'Brien, *John Bright,* p. 73.
[2] In a letter dated May 21st, 1869.
[3] An authority on Commercial Treaties; the successor of Cobden.

perceived) which gave his other faculties the order to march. These were not the most expedient qualities for a politician or a leader of politicians; but they were, after all, the qualities which have made Gladstone's name great among us. We will, in conclusion, let him speak for himself, as he did in the House of Commons on March 16th, 1868:

"If we be prudent men, I hope we shall endeavour, so far as in us lies, to make some provision for the contingencies of a doubtful and possibly dangerous future. If we be chivalrous men, I trust we shall endeavour to wipe away the stains which the civilised world has for ages seen, or seemed to see, on the shield of England in her treatment of Ireland. If we be compassionate men, I hope we shall now, once for all, listen to the tale of woe which comes from her, and the reality of which, if not its justice, is testified by the continuous migration of her people—that we shall endeavour to

'Raze out the written troubles from her brain,
Pluck from her memory the rooted sorrow'.

But above all, if we be just men, we shall go forward in the name of truth and right, bearing this in mind—that when the case is proved, and the hour is come, justice delayed is justice denied."

CHAPTER X

CONCLUSION: GLADSTONE'S DEVELOPMENT, 1859–1868

"One who never turned his back but marched breast forward."
Browning's *Epilogue*.

W E have endeavoured to trace the history of Gladstone's career from the time he took office in Lord Palmerston's Government in 1859, up to the beginning of his first premiership in 1869. The important years after the Crimean War have to be before the mind; but nothing could be found at Hawarden that was not already in the standard lives of Gladstone and of Disraeli. When Lord Derby invited Gladstone to join his administration in February, 1858, one reason he gave for declining was this: "The difficulty is even enhanced by the fact that in your party...there is a small but active and not unimportant section who avowedly regard me as the representative of the most dangerous ideas."[1] Gladstone spent an important ten years working out those dangerous ideas. We have indeed an interesting letter of 1855, which is closely applicable to his assumption of office in 1859. It is from Mr Granville Vernon,[2] a close personal friend.

"Lord Clarendon", says the letter, "is universally or nearly so looked on as essential. Next to him, I think you are considered of vital importance in your present office.

[1] Morley, *Life of Gladstone*, vol. 1, p. 578.
[2] Granville Harcourt Vernon, M.P. for Newark.

CONCLUSION

I think Sidney Herbert's presence in a cabinet is also very important. Now if Lord Palmerston attempts to form a government, I do hope that you and he will not decline to take office. After all, rightly or wrongly, Lord Palmerston is master of the situation, in the country he is looked upon as the man. If the country sees you and Sidney Herbert holding aloof from him and preventing him perhaps from forming a government, the country will blame you, and it will be said the 'Peelites' are selfish intriguers. Of course I am using the language of clubs and newspapers " (to Gladstone, February 4th, 1855).

We have quoted this " language of clubs and newspapers " for two reasons: because, between 1859 and 1865, the country still looked upon Palmerston as *the* man; and this factor made Gladstone's position one of extreme difficulty: and also because, events proved that the Peelites were not selfish intriguers. It is hardly too much to say, that the character of many statesmen of this period passes the understanding of many writers of to-day. The type of mind which Gladstone possessed is the very last which can be submitted to the now popular vogue of psychological analysis. If the character specialists have nothing more to say, than that Herbert or Gladstone or Russell were bent on gaining or keeping power, it is time for a return to archives and papers. I believe that in this period the taunt that " Victorian politics were a hot pot of opportunism "[1] can be answered by the single word "Peelites". Their most distinguished member has been the subject of this study, and the reason for the search. As Mr Bernal Osborne said on July 8th, 1864:

[1] E. H. Dance, *The Victorian Illusion*, p. 11.

"These Whig birds have been very barren and they were obliged lately to take a cross with the famous Peelite strain. I do them the justice to say, however, that there is a very great and able minister among them in the shape of a Chancellor of the Exchequer, and it is to his measures alone that they owe the little popularity and the little support which they get from this Liberal Party."[1]

We said at the outset that he would be a very foolish man who would stray far from Morley's highway. The search at Hawarden revealed, first and foremost, the greatness of the pioneer. But the letters have yielded, here and there, some of the treasure which Morley was forced to leave behind, in order to make his book manageable. On the later career of Gladstone, particularly on the first Liberal ministry, there is much of importance and value waiting for the historian.

This work was undertaken to discover by what steps Gladstone rose from being a minister to the position of the first commoner in the land; and to analyse the forces which were working upon him. During these ten years, he gained a knowledge of the people, second only to that of Bright who had spent a lifetime among them; and he acquired, in their affection and esteem, a position without parallel. The ascent was stormy, difficult and perilous; it could only have been achieved by the exercise of the "striking gift". From 1859 to 1869 he waged a ceaseless battle with traditional views and policies. On two occasions it seemed that his political life was at an end. He emerged triumphant because he exercised two great faculties; the faculty of study and the faculty of courage.

[1] Hansard, 3rd series, vol. CLXXVI.

In detail our conclusions must be these: that the "white faced, black haired man of incredible energy" was a mystery to his colleagues. Like the poet, he pondered in the night and surprised his listeners with a new ballad in the morning. On four great questions he aroused hostility; an hostility all the more bitter because it came from powerful men who had a genuine fear of change. From Cobden and Bright he received support and advice on the general question of the national expenditure, and on the particular one of the folly of huge armaments. His was the better side of the struggle, when the invasion panic of 1861 was at its height. In the last bout with Palmerston, we believe that the charges of the Prime Minister were unfounded. In 1866 and 1867, Russell and Bright were counsellors of high wisdom and courage, in the battle with Parliament and with the party. At every moment when assistance was required Bright supplied it. He did not indeed alter Gladstone's views on any great question; but he spurred him on when the pace began to flag.

The surpassing interest of this study, however, is to watch the gradual widening of Gladstone's outlook, at a time when "broadening slowly down" meant unpopularity, the mistrust of colleagues, and parliamentary embarrassment. In ten years he encountered Cabinet, leader, Parliament and party. But official dissensions were as nothing compared to his growing fame outside. The process by which he took up the cause of reform ranks with the most outstanding examples of political and personal development. In many ways it would be true to say that he had the mind of the artist. In every problem he took up, he studied detail, carefully, painfully. He passed through long stages of deliberation and rumination. At length, the great vision captured his mind; and then he went feverishly to work minutely and exhaustively. His speeches are like vast and elaborate frescoes.

This process of work, in any sphere, demands courage. In public life, only the most fearless, the most determined and the most powerful of men may attempt it, without ruining themselves and creating havoc in their surroundings. That is why we repeat, that during these ten years, Gladstone showed unflinching courage. Once the vision came, he could not deny it. He must work it out at once, however great the adversary. In his resolution, he called into action a new force in English life—a force which raised him to the highest eminence ever occupied by an English statesman—the working classes of the industrial districts. His close study of the working class, and their behaviour throughout the latter half of the nineteenth century, gave the lie direct to the idea that "the Adullamites were the best judges of Victorian democracy".[1] By 1865 the people were fit for an extension of the franchise. He, for the first time in English history, revealed to them the responsibility of an electorate.

From the end of the Crimean War to the formation of the first Gladstone Cabinet, we plot the graph of Liberalism, through three cardinal points: public economy, reform, and the Irish problem. These three subjects remained, after 1869, the main platform of the

[1] E. H. Dance, *The Victorian Illusion*, p. 35.

Liberal party. But not one of them could have been effectively and successfully met, without Gladstone. His was the bravery, the skill and the patience. Reviewing at Ormskirk some of the great measures in which he had taken an important part he said (in reference to Disraeli's assertion that he had been associated with thirty-two beneficent measures):

"There was no list given of those thirty-two measures. I do not know what they were; but gentlemen, I do know what they were not. They were not the repeal of the Roman Catholic disabilities; they were not the repeal of the disabilities of Protestant dissenters; they were not the repeal of the Corn Laws; they were not the Reform of Parliament; they were not the treaty with France; they were not that reform of the whole tariff of the country which has given you, without almost any exception, the absolute command of all the raw material of labour and industry that the world can yield without the payment of a single shilling to the exchequer."[1]

It is an impressive list; and yet few of those events with which Gladstone was connected were achieved without the utmost struggle; without foresight, knowledge, sympathy and courage. In exercising those qualities to a supreme degree Gladstone made himself the champion, if not the author, of Liberal progress in England between 1859 and 1868.

[1] At Ormskirk, December 19th, 1867.

APPENDIX

A LIST OF THE LETTERS PRINTED
FROM THE GLADSTONE PAPERS

1. Lord Clarendon *to* Gladstone. April 19th, 1853.
2. Cobden *to* Gladstone. August 5th, 1859.
3. Gladstone *to* Cobden. September 7th, 1859.
4. Cobden *to* Gladstone. October 11th, 1859.
5. Cobden *to* Gladstone. October 29th, 1859.
6. Cobden *to* Gladstone. November 11th, 1859.
7. Cobden *to* Gladstone. November 21st, 1859.
8. Cobden *to* Gladstone. November 23rd, 1859.
9. Cobden *to* Gladstone. November 29th, 1859.
10. Cobden *to* Gladstone. December 2nd, 1859.
11. Gladstone *to* Cobden. December 2nd, 1859.
12. Cobden *to* Gladstone. December 5th, 1859.
13. Cobden *to* Gladstone. December 12th, 1859.
14. Cobden *to* Gladstone. December 16th, 1859.
15. Cobden *to* Gladstone. December 23rd, 1859.
16. Gladstone *to* Cobden. January 14th, 1860.
17. Gladstone *to* Sir James Graham. January 16th, 1860.
18. Gladstone *to* Sir James Graham. November 27th, 1860.
19. Bright *to* Gladstone. April 11th, 1862.
20. Bright *to* Gladstone. August 16th, 1860.
21. Cobden *to* Gladstone. July 8th, 1860.
22. Bright *to* Gladstone. January 1st, 1861.
23. Gladstone *to* Bright. January 3rd, 1861.
24. Bright *to* Gladstone. January 9th, 1861.
25. Gladstone *to* Bright. January 15th, 1861.
26. Gladstone *to* Bright. April 15th, 1861.
27. Gladstone *to* Cobden. December 2nd, 1861.
28. Gladstone *to* Cobden. December 13th, 1861.

29. Cobden *to* Gladstone. January 12th, 1860.
30. Cobden *to* Gladstone. January 23rd, 1860.
31. Cobden *to* Gladstone. January 29th, 1860.
32. Cobden *to* Gladstone. July 2nd, 1860.
33. Cobden *to* Gladstone. December 11th, 1861.
34. Cobden *to* Gladstone. January 15th, 1862.
35. Cobden *to* Gladstone. December 19th, 1863.
36. Lord John Russell *to* Gladstone. December 7th, 1865.
37. Henry Brand *to* Gladstone. May 21st, 1864.
38. Gladstone *to* Henry Brand. May 21st, 1864.
39. Russell *to* Gladstone. January 25th, 1866.
40. Gladstone *to* Russell. October 24th, 1865.
41. Russell *to* Gladstone. January 1st, 1866.
42. Gladstone *to* Russell. January 25th, 1866.
43. Russell *to* Gladstone. January 26th, 1866.
44. Bright *to* Gladstone. February 10th, 1866.
45. Russell *to* Gladstone. February 23rd, 1866.
46. Russell *to* Gladstone. February 26th, 1866.
47. Russell *to* Gladstone. April 16th, 1866.
48. Gladstone *to* Russell. April 23rd, 1866.
49. Russell *to* Gladstone. April 30th, 1866.
50. W. E. Forster *to* Gladstone. May 11th, 1866 (with enclosure).
51. Gladstone *to* Russell. May 28th, 1866.
52. Russell *to* Gladstone. June 1st, 1866.
53. Gladstone *to* Russell. June 11th, 1866.
54. Russell *to* Gladstone. June 18th, 1866.
55. Russell *to* Gladstone. June 21st, 1866.
56. Bright *to* Gladstone. June 24th, 1866.
57. Russell *to* Gladstone. July 2nd, 1866.
58. Russell *to* Gladstone. July 3rd, 1866.
59. Gladstone *to* Sir J. Fremantle. June 23rd, 1866.
60. Robert Lowe *to* Gladstone. March 21st, 1867.
61. Bright *to* Gladstone. May 11th, 1867.
62. Bright *to* Gladstone. July 31st, 1867.

LIST OF LETTERS

63. Bright *to* Gladstone. December 9th, 1867.
64. Gladstone *to* Bright. December 10th, 1867.
65. H. C. E. Childers *to* Gladstone. January 15th, 1868.
66. W. E. Forster *to* Gladstone. March 22nd, 1868.
67. Marquis of Hartington *to* Gladstone. October 1st, 1868.
68. Bright *to* Gladstone. November 27th, 1868.
69. Bright *to* Gladstone. July 30th, 1869.
70. G. E. H. Vernon *to* Gladstone. February 4th, 1855.

INDEX

187

INDEX

INDEX

Ormskirk, 81, 106, 145, 163, 182
Oxford, 108

Palmerston, Lord, on Baines's Bill, 93–9; on Commercial Treaty, 30; on danger from France, 41, 45, 54; effects of death of, 111–17; relations with Gladstone (1860–1), 36–57
Paper Duty Repeal, 35, 36, 41, 43, 56
Peel, Sir Robert, 4, 22, 26, 35, 53, 106, 137, 162
Peelites, the, 178
Pitt, William (the Younger), 17, 137
Potteries, the, 103–4
Press, influence and character of, 4–5, 42–3, 57
Preston, 172
Punch, 37, 88

Reform, Agitation for, 74–81, 91–7, 100
Reform Bill (1866), 127–42
Reform Bill (1867), 147–57
Rochdale, 154
Rosebery, Lord, 10, 121
Rouher, M., 24–6, 28–30
Ruskin, J., 70–1

Russell, Lord John, Reform Bill (1866), 118–19, 125–42; retirement, 142; otherwise mentioned, 2, 27, 39, 47
— Lord John, Letters from: on Reform Bill (1866), 118, 127, 129–30
on Liberalism, 142

St Helens, 168
Selborne, Lord (Sir R. Palmer), *Memorials* quoted, 14–15, 108, 147, 159
Southport, 160
Staffordshire Sentinel, 104

Times, The, 42–4, 60, 80
Torrens, McCullagh, 124
Townsend, M., 12, 15

Vernon, G. H., Letter to Gladstone, 177–8
Victoria, Queen, 113, 118, 134–5, 137–9, 150, 166

Walewski, Count, 25
Wellington, Duke of, 66, 121
West, Sir Algernon, 12–13
Wood, Sir Charles, 111, 127

York, 110

For EU product safety concerns, contact us at Calle de José Abascal, 56–1°, 28003 Madrid, Spain or eugpsr@cambridge.org.

www.ingramcontent.com/pod-product-compliance
Ingram Content Group UK Ltd.
Pitfield, Milton Keynes, MK11 3LW, UK
UKHW020316140625
459647UK00018B/1901